BEYOND
BAT & BALL

Eleven Intimate
Portraits

BEYOND
BAT & BALL

Eleven Intimate Portraits

DAVID FOOT

Foreword
by
Dennis Silk

AURUM PRESS

*To Anne, who used to rock the pram while
dictating my cricket copy from the nearest
phone box*

*And Darrell Wood, my English
master, a Yorkshireman and cricketer, who
helped me to appreciate words and cover drives*

First published in a limited edition 1993
by Good Books (GB Publications Ltd).
This trade edition first published 1995
by Aurum Press Limited,
25 Bedford Avenue, London, WC1B 3AT.

A catalogue record for this book is available
from the British Library.

ISBN 1 85410 339 3

Printed and bound in Great Britain
by Hartnolls Ltd, Bodmin

CONTENTS

FOREWORD
by *Dennis Silk, President of MCC* 9

INTRODUCTION 13

ONE
WILFRED WOOLLER: *That Bloody Wilf Wooller* 17

TWO
SIEGFRIED SASSOON: *Inner Peace at Mid-on* 37

THREE
JACK FINGLETON: *Radical with a Taste for Toffs* 53

FOUR
BILL ANDREWS: *Twelve O'Clock Low* 71

FIVE
ANDY DUCAT: *A Fitting Exit* 89

SIX
BILL GRESWELL: *Talent Unfulfilled* 105

SEVEN
JIM SMITH: *Big Heart and Biceps* 123

EIGHT
BEV LYON: *Visionary with a Yellow Rolls-Royce* 139

NINE
BERTIE POORE: *Play Interrupted by Boers* 157

TEN
JACK MERCER: *Bowler with an Ace up his Sleeve* 171

ELEVEN
TOM RICHARDSON: *A Game Too Many* 187

BIBLIOGRAPHY 199

INDEX 201

ACKNOWLEDGEMENTS

I start with Dennis Silk, thanking him for his most generous preface, and for the help he gave me in my research over the chapter on Siegfried Sassoon. My gratitude is extended to Rupert Hart-Davis, Sassoon's literary executor, for permission to quote from 'Dreamers', from *Counter-Attack and other Poems* (Heinemann, 1918).

It was at least possible to go to source in the case of Wilfred Wooller; he gave both time and useful self-analysis. All my other subjects are dead. But I was able to talk at length to relatives and friends, to be shown in some cases private correspondence and to be made privy to domestic confidences. All those I spoke to were, without exception, honest in their appraisal.

My contacts were wide-ranging: from the politician (The Rt Hon The Lord Howell, previously Denis Howell, MP) to the marvellous old cricketers (like Dennis Brookes and Andy Wilson); from the cleric (Father Martin of Downside) to the cricket writers (John Woodcock, Matthew Engel, Scyld Berry and Andy Radd). I thank them all, as I do past and present occupants of the scorebox like Ted Lester and Clem Driver.

I come, with equal gratitude, to the various relatives and intimates. They include Ennyd Andrews and her children Mark and Sara; Daphne Cowderoy and Dr Tony Barbour; Mrs Rachel Greswell, Mrs Gill Goodland, John and Jeaff Greswell; David Smith (Jim's son); Mrs Rosemary Richardson and, indirectly, her son, the late Ed Poore who always wanted me to write about his illustrious uncle.

My thank-you list seems to be endless. There are John Luff, Stephen Green, custodian of Lord's excellent library, those ever-helpful statisticians, David Smith (Wiltshire) and Keith Ball (Bristol)... And others, almost at random: John Ruddick, Roy Newman, Tony Ellis and Simon Wotton.

The photographs have come from various sources: Bristol United Press, Glamorgan CCC, David Frith, Press Association, relatives and friends. Thank you all.

AUTHOR'S NOTE

The composition of my team has been a private indulgence. I have wanted to write about most of them for a long time. Almost all were exceptional players in their various ways: by vibrant leadership, warm-heartedness, quirks and fearful insecurity in some cases, and of course often innate brilliance on the field. One, Siegfried Sassoon, may even have been a rotten cricketer by conventional standards; but his enthusiasm could be mesmeric during those matches in a Wiltshire meadow. They offered the sweetest of havens as gnawing thoughts and images of the trenches temporarily receded. The book has been written with much affection as I have searched to explain the whole man, not merely eleven individual cricketers.

FOREWORD

How Siegfried Sassoon would revel in opening the innings with Wilf Wooller, and how Bill Andrews would chuckle at promotion to No 4, ahead of Bev Lyon and Bertie Poore. They might be forgiven for scowling at their relegation to eight and nine in the order respectively. But this is a book about much more than cricket, as David Foot is quick to indicate. In each of the enchanting essays we are taken far 'beyond bat and ball' into the minds and indeed the hearts of the subjects.

If the cricket lover is not quite clear about why he loves the game, he will become much clearer after reading this book. The psychology of the game and its players is explored with real insight and sympathy by a writer who comes closer to the lyric prose of Robertson-Glasgow than anyone I have read for twenty years.

'Cricket', said a great West Indian wicket-keeper to me in my Cambridge salad days, 'is like a woman: you either love it or hate it'. Each of these players was, in one sense or another, a victim of fate, of talent stunted by lack of opportunity or progress barred by ill-disposed selectors. Wilf Wooller was the prisoner of the Japanese when, in happier times, he might have been knocking on the door for the England captaincy. Bill Greswell was sent off to plant tea in Ceylon when he might have been doing to the Australian batsmen and bowlers what all healthy young Englishmen long to do. Andy Ducat hit fifty-two hundreds for Surrey but won only one England cap in a match which saw him dismissed when his bat was shattered in his hand by a fiery lifter. A splinter from the bat's shoulder fell on the stumps and dislodged a bail. Surrey got rid of him for 'reasons of economy' only a year after he had scored 2,000 runs for them in a season. Bertie Poore, learning to bat from books and pamphlets in India, enjoyed phenomenal success for Hampshire before his military duties took him off to the South African war and obscurity. Here was the prototype all-round sportsman. Between pig-sticking and polo, rackets and tiger shooting, he scored a multitude of centuries. His military training had produced a thoroughly well-organised man and he needed to be to find time in so many fields of physical endeavour.

Much of the book takes us down to the West Country where even the charming but tough and acerbic Australian, Jack Fingleton, felt at home in rural Somerset. Who wouldn't at the generous table of the Mendip Quarryman John Luff? What can have induced the depressions to which Bill Andrews was subject, one wonders, in the happy festival atmosphere of Weston-super-Mare? He gave his heart and soul to Somerset cricket but he cried out for recognition and friendship. In tandem with Arthur Wellard he became an integral part of the Somerset legend, but the black shadow of melancholia haunted him all the way to the grave, a deeply complex and tragic figure for all the jovial banter and convivial drinking the world expected of him.

It is at Weston that David Foot provides us with a vivid vignette of gentle Jack Mercer performing his conjuring tricks on the bonnet of a car in passing through the car park on the way to the scorebox, giving his commentary in 'embarrassingly amplified tones that suggested his hearing-aid wasn't switched on'. Here was a mystery man who loved racing, spoke French and Russian, mastered the *Times* crossword daily in five minutes and had worked for intelligence in the war. He played a little for Sussex and Hampshire and became a pillar of Glamorgan before ending his days with Northants as coach and scorer for thirty-six years. His bowling could easily have been used by England: accurate, rhythmical and liable to swing either way. But he will be remembered best for his many kindnesses to struggling players, and for his deep and unfailing love of the game to which he had given a lifetime's service.

—

Big Jim Smith was about as different to Jack Mercer as it was possible to be. Fine fast bowler though he was, he will be remembered far more for his big hitting than for his bowling. Not even Ian Botham emptied the bars more swiftly when he went out to bat than did Jim Smith. In his Wiltshire homespun manner, he entertained as few have done before or since. A fifty at Bristol in 1938 took him all of eleven minutes. Batting with Hammond in the West Indies, he overshadowed his great partner by scoring 83 of the 122 they added together. But at heart he remained a farmer, a son of the soil with all the decent simple values one would expect of a Wiltshire yeoman. He loved to feed his animals and was most at peace in his smallholding, even after he became a publican. There was about him, even when he was playing at Lord's, a flavour of the ale house, the village green and the hay field.

Tom Richardson was another great fast bowler who ended his life as a publican. Fast bowling made an old man of him in his early thirties and the swift obscurity which settles so cruelly soon on so many cricketers was made more painful for him by the defection of his wife. He had worn himself out for his county and his country and life seemed to have lost its purpose. Moreover he was wracked by rheumatism. When he was found dead on a country path in France the whispers went about that he had taken his own life. Leaving the first-class stage with all its companionship, its adulation and its mutual support can be a traumatic experience for those with limited interests and narrow horizons.

Those who love cricket will revel in this book. In a sense it solves the conundrum of why the game remains the only game that has provided us with a great literature. This book proves, if proof were needed, that the game is far more about people and their personalities than it is about their feats. The authors who last are those whose real interests lie with the people rather than with the statistics they produce. Success and failure mould character, to be

—

sure, but the subtleties and the complexities of cricket provide a background so rich in its diversity and so demanding in its disciplines that it builds character in a way that no other game can match. Sassoon, the poet of war, could dream that he was Woolley and learn to live with the waking knowledge that he was not. Bertie Poore could score 304 for Hampshire and take the next match off to play polo. Bill Greswell settled down to grow his raspberries in Williton in the sure knowledge that exile in Ceylon had robbed him of England caps.

The challenge is always there for each man to solve in his own peculiar way. The game is apt to make philosophers of us all, and how these philosophies made or broke these particular men gives us a fascinating insight into the human condition.

Dennis Silk.

INTRODUCTION

This is not really a book about cricket. All my eleven subjects were fine players in their different ways - and there are many sources of reference for those who want to garnish with soulless statistics or relive golden summers.

My fascination for cricket has always extended beyond the playing field, beyond bat and ball, and I have long contended that, unlike most other sports, it is played just as much with the capricious mind. That is why I have tried, at the risk of sounding pretentious, to make this for the most part a miscellany of psychological studies.

Some of my chosen sportsmen were under-praised during their careers. Not all, and Wilf Wooller would agree, were unfailingly loved. My self-imposed brief was to interpret, against a canvas of the first-class game, the way a number of them were burdened by complexes and torments, about which the general public were quite unaware. Throughout this book runs a thread of warmth. I saw few of my 'team' play and met only seven of them; but I like to think I watched and admired all of them.

They are fully worthy of reassessment and retrospective praise. It is not simply geographical allegiance that convinces me Bev Lyon should have captained England at least once (yet could the po-faced establishment have risked him?). Who knows what Major Poore might have achieved if he hadn't gone back to fight the Boers - or how many Test appearances there would have been for Bill Greswell if he hadn't been sent off, against his will, to help with the tea planting in Ceylon?

Greswell, a brilliant debutant for Somerset after leaving Repton, was one of the innovators of in-swing bowling. He also scored a hundred on his first visit with the county to Lord's. The Test selectors were already noting his precocious skills and marking him down as a certainty for England recognition. All he wanted from life, for his part, was to play cricket. The career, cruelly predetermined for him, was an acrid let-down. He ended as Somerset's president, a lean, diffident figure walking the boundary at Taunton with unseeing eyes.

The spectators idolised so many of the players in the following pages, yet seldom knowing what was going on in their minds. How many had any inkling of the mental demons that kept returning, every spring, to depress and hound Bill Andrews, the most flamboyant and amusing of cricketers? Somerset was the county of Percy Hardy, Raymond Robertson-Glasgow and Harold Gimblett. They all, in the end, found life too much for them. Three times, Bill Andrews confided: 'Don't worry, I won't top myself'. But during his numerous black periods, and latterly as he became increasingly a recluse, he admitted it crossed his mind recurrently. He was possibly saved by a devoted family. Suicide can't be avoided in my chapter on that wonderful Romany bowler, Tom Richardson. Others have researched diligently and eventually concluded that he died in France of natural causes. But the circumstances of his death were disturbingly enigmatic. There were many regrets in the last few years of this warm-hearted fast bowler's life. One was surely his last abortive first-class appearance, away from Surrey. It was a painful mockery of his wondrous talents.

All is not gloom, I assure you. In Wooller's case, I set out to find a reason for the less endearing traits of this man of courage, dogmatic assertion, and Taff Tyranny. Future generations will come to appreciate fully his influence on Glamorgan cricket. He, too, like Lyon, should have skippered England. Many experiences moulded him: I look again in this book at the effects of the cultural remoteness, over the mountains, of the North Walean schoolboy - and the ghastly repercussions of being a prisoner of the Japanese.

Andy Ducat, who died at Lord's with a bat in his hand, was the

—

most delightful of Surrey cricketers. He also led out, in shimmering claret and blue, Aston Villa in the FA Cup Final. Andy played for England at both sports and I feel we have been remiss in our seemingly scant regard for his considerable, if unostentatious, dual abilities.

Cricket is also, of course, a game which hums with humour. I went back to the small Wiltshire town where Big Jim Smith first brandished that unsubtle blade of his. No one at Middlesex or in the West Indies, where in no time he toured under R.E.S. Wyatt, ever said an uncharitable word about him. I chuckled, at firsthand, at the acerbic wit of Jack Fingleton - and enjoyed the droll asides of Jack Mercer as he spontaneously went into his latest conjuring trick on the bonnet of a parked car.

Siegfried Sassoon is the odd man out. He may not have played county cricket but he knew the initials of every pre-war amateur; he read the cricket scores in *The Times* before breakfast, and turned out with regularity for his village team at Heytesbury. He loved cricket more than the hunting field. I have long wanted to write something about his cricket, not least the way he seemed impervious to bruised shins as he indolently, comically, stationed himself at mid-on.

In compiling these portraits, I have in a number of cases gone back to my subjects' homes, walked the country lanes they walked in my search for the authentic ambience, talked to their close relatives, descendants and friends. Without exception, I have understood my eleven cricketers better by the end and liked them even more. I hope you will share my affection for them.

ONE

WILF WOOLLER

That Bloody Wilf Wooller

———

Wooller, Wilfred. Born Rhos-on-Sea, Denbighshire, 1912. All-rounder and brilliant close fielder. Cambridge University (1935-36; blue both years); Glamorgan (1938-62, 400 matches). Captained county 1947-60 and was Secretary until 1978. Played rugby for Cambridge University, Cardiff and Wales.

BY ONE OF THOSE STRANGE, felicitous coincidences, I found myself doing my RAF reserve training alongside that talented, if impulsive, Glamorgan all-rounder, Jim Pressdee. We had adjoining beds and he kept me amused, before we got off to sleep, with stories of his brief career at the Vetch, where once he had hoped to establish himself as a successful league footballer for Swansea Town. In those days an eager, young journalist, who avidly read about rather than reported the deeds of professional sportsmen, I was far more enthralled by what he had to say in his sleep.

Twice, during our fortnight's training, he woke me with an unmistakable oath. 'That bloody Wilf Wooller . . .'

Others in the billet heard him. One or two taxed, or rather teased, him with it next morning. His typically West Glamorgan face, with its strong jaw, reacted in disbelief. Jim's cousin, who by some quirk of fate in the way reservists were chosen had found himself in the same wooden hut, opted for tact and loyalty. He had heard nothing. But you somehow felt he didn't rule it out completely.

As a mild insomniac, I used to listen with unwavering fascination to the surreal elements of night language and even became something of an authority on the subject of talking in one's sleep, during my National Service days. The supposedly lascivious utterances of Fred Trueman, at Padgate the week before me, remained a talking point long after he had left for his square-bashing station. At a combined services camp at Coulsdon, where for six months I wrestled with the Russian language, a withdrawn and pious graduate from Keble College who was planning to enter the Church when his conscription was over, went into regular nocturnal tirades. It was not unusual for a dozen of us to sit up in bed, mesmerised by the sheer obscenity of his monologues. They were magnificent misanthropy, interwoven with the most basic of Anglo-Saxon adornments. The voice was different; it was as if he'd taken on another persona altogether. As far as I know, no one ever dared tell him.

Jim Pressdee's voice was his own, true and picturesque as his native Mumbles. Later, as I came to study the history of Glamorgan, I understood better the apparent disaffection contained in the words he directed unknowingly at his county captain in the dead of night.

Wooller admired many of the combative qualities of a player who, when he decided on a whim to emigrate to South Africa at the age of thirty-two, had taken nearly 500 wickets, scored well over 13,000 runs and held on to 343 catches. But the pair sparred, at times publicly. Their differences, impetuous and in retrospect amusing, seemed one of the accepted strands of high drama in a Glamorgan season.

'What's that row going on in Wilf's office?'

'Him and Jim going hammer and tongs.'

Some of the pros approved of the manner Pressdee stood up to the authoritative and often intimidating Wooller. No one would have ever called him a sycophant. 'You're a cheeky bugger, Jim,' they would say, a glint of envy in their eyes. 'Got to stick up to Wilf - or he'll ride all over you,' he would reply, the step firm and defiant as he moved away from the secretary's office.

Wooller could have big rows, that was the nature of the man. He was a martinet. His wrath was not reserved for the weak. He would be just as likely to unleash a diatribe at a prevaricating committee man as one of the more militant members of his team.

I recently asked him about his relationship with Pressdee. 'Ah yes, he was a pig-headed so and so. We had our differences, both when I was captain and secretary. I remember matches when he was being hit through mid-wicket. He'd ask me to put a fielder there. But I wouldn't give way to him.

'Pitch that ball on the right spot and that batsman won't be able to get you away like that. And if he hits you for four boundaries there in the next over, you still won't have a fielder there, I'd tell him. Pressdee hated being punished and it worked.'

There were various smouldering contretemps, not just with that strong-minded all-rounder. It wasn't difficult for the spectators at the Arms Park or St Helen's to detect it. The anger showed in the Wooller stride between the overs. He made no great attempt, at any time, to hide his displeasure. On occasions, his oaths would reach the boundary faster than a Parkhouse cover drive. He kicked backsides with all the vigour one would expect from boots that once landed long-range penalties with meaty precision. He didn't know what it meant to pussyfoot. Opponents with formidable reputations, amateurs and professionals, were subjected to his ire. He was less than enchanted with the executive skills of a sweeping range of Glamorgan officials, including Ossie Wheatley and Bill Edwards at some time or other, and he expressed his feelings without a hint of ambiguity. He spoke his mind with an assertiveness that implied the sheer futility of a challenge. Wilf fired off his opinions with the autocratic air of finality one heard from crusty Edwardian county skippers. The difference was that, apart from leading by example himself, his words were usually bolstered by logic and the best of intentions.

He hated cant and intrigue. There were times when, as secretary, he was not privy to the Celtic politicking. The way A.E.Burnett, the Eton housemaster, had been surreptitiously sounded-out as likely captain of Glamorgan - he was registered without Wooller's knowledge - appeared to him as an outrage. John Clay resigned. Amid all the turmoil of Glamorgan cricket in the late Fifties, Wilf offered his resignation and later withdrew it.

Like most of the bitterest internecine battles, that have punctuated the history of county cricket, many of the arguments at Glamorgan were petty and personal. As Wooller was to write in his history of the county:

—

Both sides held councils of war behind suitably entrenched positions. One erring committee man had to have a writ slapped on him because he was letting it be quietly understood in certain public quarters that I had been milking the expenses. The flies of the major sports clubs were, with relish, assassinating my private character, notwithstanding the fact that I had an exceedingly attractive wife and was clearly very happily married . . .

He never once in his life recoiled from a fight when he felt that a principle was at stake. His enemies, not a negligible number because of the nature of the man, always conceded he was supported by moral as well as physical courage. The unflinching low tackles at the Arms Park, the catches he took at forward short leg from ferocious pulls, the resilience of the war years, combine to reflect the intrepid strands of his seemingly aggressive and at times misunderstood personality.

The words of LAC Pressdee, cumulative though dreamy in his case, were echoed in committee rooms. 'That bloody Wooler' . . . I heard it first when I eavesdropped near the visiting members' deckchairs in front of the claustrophobic pavilion at Weston's Clarence Park, where Glamorgan were Somerset's opponents. I had no idea whether it was a general opinion - or a fair one. Only in retrospect can one realise the effects all those taunts, not always quite out of earshot, had on a reasonably well-proportioned ego. He eventually stepped down as secretary after thirty-one years of conscientious and at times contentious service. 'They were probably glad to see the back of me,' he told me with an endearing twinkle.

He had taken over as captain in 1947, to become one of the undeniable autocrats of county cricket. His influence on Glamorgan is immense; so is his affection for the club and the successive generations who played with and for him, some it must be accepted in various degrees of fear. He would, of course, pooh-pooh the

—

notion. 'There had to be discipline. Yes, of course I was abrasive up to a point, but it was psychologically applied. If catches went down, I never once ticked off the offender on the field. But when I considered we had had a bad day, I ordered everyone in for a special practice session at half-past nine next morning.' The corporate groans united the disparate geographical elements in the team: Swansea and Cardiff was ever an uneasy marriage, except when a rebuke was being issued. Wooller himself was from North Wales; it gave objectivity to his punitive powers.

He ruled the field, as skipper, and seldom called for a second opinion. 'I wanted to win - I was born a competitive creature. And I expected my team to accept my orders. It was very different off the field. I liked to live and drink beer with my players. They could say what they liked, criticise as much as they wished. I didn't inhibit them.'

Indeed, at the right time, he liked to be, and to be seen as, one of the boys. The after-match session with a round of drinks came no doubt from his rugby days. He enjoyed the mutual teasing, cricketing tales that got embroidered as the night wore on. In his pre-war sporting days, he was a willing initiate to the occasional extramural activity, one of which involved a hasty and miscalculated retreat through a cucumber frame. One old pro also warmly remembered the collective drinking sessions when Wooller was in charge of the team. 'You saw a different side of him - he could be great fun. He loved to hear the timeless Welsh stories. But, knowing him, he usually had more to say than anyone.'

That was probably a fair point. As a conversational monopolist, he had few equals. Press-box colleagues, in the days when he was working for the *News Chronicle* or later the *Daily* and *Sunday Telegraph*, could be bombarded with his opinions on the game, or the state of the Nation. He was always dogmatic, always articulate. I graphically remember the first time I was sitting in the box at

—

Sophia Gardens when he came in to pay us a social visit. It was coming up to edition time and after the initial greeting, everyone around me suddenly became preoccupied with their prose. Wilf, maybe sensing that he had no obvious audience, started throwing a few technical questions about the day's play into the pipe-smoky air.

I fell for it. Genuinely interested in one of the points he clearly wanted to make, I responded with a pretty bland view of my own. He immediately came and sat next to me and for the next twenty minutes he talked. There was no scope for a duologue. As far as I recall at this distance, it was one of his discourses on swing bowling. It made eminent sense; this was his specialist subject after all. The manner was inclined to be donnish but it was a valuable part of my education. Then, his tutorial completed, he left. One felt the lesson on swing bowling was intended for all of us.

A Welsh friend turned to me and screwed up his face eloquently. 'Brave of you, boyo. We know the signs when Wilf looks in so we get on with our work. He loves a bloody audience . . .'

After that, whenever we met, we seemed to get on quite well, though I doubt if he knew who I was. I have always been a listener, a distinct advantage in any extended 'conversation' with him. One teatime at Bristol, where we were covering the match between Gloucestershire and Hampshire for rival papers, he invited me down to the bar. He was by then into his seventies but looking ten years younger. He led the way with distinctive long strides, head jogging up and down. We drank pints and I remember thinking how affable he was. In a way it bothered me. I'd seen him on a previous occasion being deliberately argumentative and, worse, bigoted. Once he had come into a crowded press box, which contained at the time an Asian journalist, and made the kind of sweeping remark about black cricketers that left me, and I am sure the Asian, feeling embarrassed. Maybe he hadn't spotted our Indian guest; but that didn't excuse the gist of his observation.

—

In the bar, during the tea interval at Bristol back in the early Eighties, he was a companion of infinite charm. There was no trivia in his conversation; he had no time for it. He extolled the virtues of David Gower at some length. He talked indirectly of his gradual eclipse from Glamorgan, and didn't really succeed in hiding his regrets. His tanned face brightened when he manoeuvred the subject matter to bowls, which he had taken up recently - presumably to fill the void - with all the passion once devoted to rugby football and cricket. I need not have feared that he would unleash, at any moment in that booming voice of his, one of his more contentious observations.

That evening I came to the conclusion that he had mellowed: so much so, in fact, that I actually asked him to cover for me to do a cricket report for *The Guardian* on a day when I was taken ill. Wooller writing for *The Guardian*, a radical organ which represented many of the values which he supposedly despised? He had no qualms - and turned in a nice, straight 400 words, devoid blissfully of any of his more trenchant phobias. The next time I saw him and thanked him for standing in, he said: 'First time I've ever written for your lot, you know. They put it in just as I wrote it. But I must say I was very glad they didn't use my name in the paper. That would never have done.'

I smiled to myself. He'd clearly obtained a *Guardian* to check his report. It would hardly have done, of course, if a local newsagent had recognised him on his surreptitious dalliance with this purveyor of gently lefty notions. Maybe he persuaded his delightful wife to don a suitable disguise in making the modest Wooller purchase.

On my visit to his Cardiff home, at the time of a general election, there were Conservative posters conspicuously displayed in the front garden. 'But it would be wrong to call me a person of extreme right-wing views. No, not extreme.' That impression emanated no doubt from the militant days of Peter Hain and his orchestrated campaign to stop the South African rugby tour of this country. Wooller championed the cause of South African sport vociferously: on radio, television and, if necessary, public platform. The opinions were unequivocal and carried a seemingly reactionary zeal. It didn't mean he was pro-apartheid, he used to say.

In 1970 he took part in a televised debate from the Cambridge Union on the question of South Africa and sport. He teamed up with Ted Dexter; the motion, that political commitment shouldn't intrude upon sporting contacts, was opposed by John Arlott and the then Minister of Sport, Denis Howell.

Wooller reminded his audience that he'd played with and against 'that great and lovable sportsman Learie Constantine' before the war, at a time when the West Indian was being refused admission to one of our leading hotels. Sport, he said, was opposed to racialism and to the apartheid system, but he didn't believe that it alone could change things. It was not a particularly memorable debate. But the evening belonged essentially to the simple, stirring oratory of Arlott, who spoke with barely a glance at his notes for a quarter of an hour. It was Arlott, the old-fashioned Liberal, who swayed the voting. The motion was defeated decisively.

All through his sporting life, Wooller has irritated and exasperated those who take an opposing attitude, whether about the state of the game, the polls or the international climate. Yet no one would question his intellectual integrity. He doesn't compromise. Nor has he mellowed, he assures me with instant vigour in the riposte. That is not my present-day assessment, but I stifle a challenge. From my limited intimate knowledge of the man, already an irascible and retrospectively loved legend of Welsh sport, I am much more enamoured of the softer bowls-playing version. 'Come on out into the garden. Another of my hobbies, you know.' Can it really be the so-called erstwhile raging tyrant of county cricket?

He always looked on himself, whatever the rigidly imposed

structures on the playing field, as a convivial fellow. Would he consider himself classless? Indeed he would. 'Listen, one or two of my best friends who played rugby for Cardiff came from the labouring classes. Before the war, I used to invite them along to the Squash Club. They'd never been into a place like that before. I have always judged a person not by his social standing but by what he is.'

That's the appeal of the man, less so the unabated vigour of his language on the field. The air was often blue when Wilf, six foot two inches of honest sweat and combative enthusiasm, straddled the action. 'There was always effing and blinding. But that was the era in which we played - and it was forgotten the moment you were off the field. You should have heard R.W.V.Robins . . . Yes, and what about Worcestershire's noble lord?'

He was talking of the Hon Charles Lyttleton, later to be the 10th Viscount Cobham, on the day in the late Thirties when he was captaining his county against Glamorgan. Wooller was playing: during a fortnight's holiday from his job in the coal industry. From the pavilion, his pads already off, he heard and shared the Welsh guffaws. It was a considerable extension of his descriptive vocabulary, acquired from eavesdropping at centre threequarter. 'The forwards used to belt each other and the backs were the gentlemen of the game,' he would say. Was Wilf, one must ask, really one of rugby football's decorously silent gentlemen? It's hard to credit, knowing the range of his cricketing linguistics. But back to Lyttleton.

'It looked as though Worcestershire were going to win by an innings. Even more so when Jack Mercer, our No 10, gave a straightforward catch to mid-off. But my noble lord put it down. Jack decided it was his day - and he began to hit six after six off poor Dick Howorth. Suddenly we'd saved the match. Charles Lyttleton, in some anger, conceded a draw by hurling the stumps into the air. The words he used, I promise you, would have earned unstinted praise from a Cardiff docker.'

That memory stirred others. One was the much-publicised incident in the early Fifties when Reg Simpson, increasingly irked by Wooller's obduracy on the placid Trent Bridge wicket, started bowling underarm to him after tea. There couldn't have been a more blatant battle-cry. Compounded scowls and acidulous words were exchanged freely. On the boundaries, maiden aunts and small children were no doubt told to put their hands over their ears. Poor Willie Jones found the taut atmosphere too much for him and got himself out, to heighten his skipper's wrath. Nottinghamshire would have to pay for that. Wooller swore, scowled even more - and batted on till lunchtime on the following day. 'That was something Glamorgan rarely did.'

It was popularly believed that Wooller and Simpson viewed each other with regular disaffection. 'Certainly not so. We got on well, whatever the public may have thought.' Another case, he seemed to imply, of the public and press getting it wrong: of judging him solely by his visible outbursts, failing to appreciate that the blood did not run hot for long and that he didn't harbour grievances.

Nor does Andy Wilson, one of Gloucestershire's best and smallest wicket-keepers. He confirms the tale reluctantly, still a little shocked that it happened at all. Glamorgan were the opponents - and Wooller, accurate medium pace with some movement that day, was bowling at Wilson. Arthur Milton was the batsman at the other end. 'Andy was chopping and edging them through gully and the slips. Wilf was getting more and more enraged, especially when a catch at last went straight to slip and he dropped it.'

Glamorgan's desperately frustrated captain went striding down the wicket to confront a batsman who seemed chest-high to him. Milton recalls: 'Wilf looked straight at Andy and called him 'a ——— lucky little bastard.'

—

Wilson was by nature an introvert, a man of quiet charm and a sense of propriety. He thought well of people and walked away from controversy. On this occasion, he was roused to response. It isn't certain which of the words galvanised him most. 'Mr Wooller, is that what they taught you at Cambridge?'

Andy laughs about it now and bears no obvious grudge. In his post-playing days as a fully paid-up NUJ cricket writer, he must have shared a press box with Wilf on occasions. The reflective long-range view of Milton is also significant. 'I'd have played for Wilf . . . anytime. For all his rages, he was a fair man.'

In any study of Wilfred Wooller, I come back recurrently to the sheer dichotomy of the personality - the bigot and the beer-drinking democrat, the argumentative sportsman and the charmer, the rather fearsome figure and the sentimental family man, the big, physical animal and the intellectual. Not all the labels can be fully validated.

I'd heard all about 'that bloody Wilf Wooller' long before I met him. But what made him seemingly go out of his way at times to embrace polemics and to express sentiments that made headlines rather than help him court popularity? Could there have been a lurking sense of the dramatic, a mischievous relish to upset apple carts?

It seems to be unchallengeable that he has been largely moulded by the isolated ambience, in the psychological as well as in the geographical and political meaning, of where he was born. Talk to him at length of his early days in North Wales. He comes back repeatedly to the fact that 'we were cut off' . . . that 'there was no real contact between us and the people in South Wales' . . . that 'we were a very different breed, on our own, more Welsh.'

He would, romantically if not realistically, have liked to see an All-Welsh team representing Glamorgan. Yet interestingly he doesn't speak Welsh and always insisted that his players communicate in English.

—

His father had been a builder. As a boy, Wilf spent hours on his own: fishing, swimming, doing physical things. There was no great social grandeur. He was sent to Rydal but didn't really want to go - because it played rugby and not soccer. Around his home, near the coast in Denbighshire, he was an energetic footballer, rampaging through the middle as a centre forward. He had the kick of a mule and the goals multiplied. It isn't often remembered that when he came to South Wales to work, he signed briefly for Cardiff City and played a league game against Fulham. Just another strand in the confusing pattern of his life.

The Wooller roots may have been English but the temperament belonged to that of the North Walean. There was an innately defensive mechanism, a short fuse or, conversely, a long glare of defiance. I asked him for his initial reaction when he moved south. 'I found them down there more open-minded. Very easy to mix with. A friendly people.' He had arrived in all ignorance, arguably a victim of the great cultural divide. I got the firm impression that it came as a surprise to him.

But the influence of his growing-up at Colwyn Bay tells less than half the story, I feel, of how this dominant, dogmatic man emerged. All the evidence suggests that his four years as a Japanese prisoner-of-war hold the key of his ambiguous character. 'I was a guest of the Japanese and I can find nothing good or gracious to say about them - they were a bestial crowd.'

His weight went down from fourteen to eleven stone. There were deprivations, the hardships and the boredom. There was also, for him, time to think. 'This was when I became a capitalist,' he says in absolute seriousness.

'We did what we could to add to our meagre rations. That meant gardening. And this was when I learned so much about human nature. We were living in what was really a communist system - everything was pooled and shared. It became obvious to me that about a third of the men were prepared to work for the good of the community. A third did it if they were ordered to. The remainder did as little as possible but expected to get their share from anything going. I hadn't bothered at all with politics before the war. Now I saw that unless you provided a carrot, the average individual was not likely to give of his best . . .'

I doubt whether Wooller's grim experience at the hands of the Japanese simply moulded him politically. Sub-consciously, it possibly left him with a wary, maybe unloving regard for cultures and races very different from his own. I don't know whether he has ever bought a Japanese car but I should think it is unlikely.

No badly treated POW comes out of his experiences unscathed. It must be hard not to feel a lingering bitterness: even harder not to take on a corrosive layer of cynicism. The human spirit has been severely tested. Which of us can say with certainty that some of the apparent tantrums and less charitable actions of cricketer Wooller were not attributable to those demeaning months and years after his capture.

They also made him, he tells you, a more rounded person. There were lessons to be learned. He watched with undimmed admiration the way that some prisoners, all skin and bone, could carry enormous weights on their backs over twenty miles or so. 'They just kept going - and it taught me so much about what was possible with a common resolve and determination.'

It wasn't only capitalism that took shape for him during his years as a prisoner. He pondered many aspects of the human condition: the work ethic, the need, as he saw it, of driving the others hard, leadership and respect. He came home after the war a very different man, not just thinner.

The coal industry was coming up to nationalisation and he was advised to look elsewhere. Gradually cricket became his life, though at first hardly his living. He needed to supplement his modest earnings as Glamorgan's secretary with work as a sports writer and broadcaster. As an amateur player and skipper - he seemed to be known by everyone in the Principality as 'Skipper' - some of the philosophies he'd acquired while under the unpleasant oppression of the Japanese took discernible shape. He convinced fairly average Glamorgan sides that they could be exceptional ones. He drove them with bullish venom on a tightrope of psychology that would dissolve, just in time, amid the pipe smoke of the communal evening bar, into gales of shared laughter.

'I also used to remember how before the war Glamorgan appeared to accept that they wouldn't beat counties like Yorkshire. The idea was to make sure the game lasted for three days and see that at least we got some money through the gate. I just couldn't understand that defeatist attitude. Now I saw my job as having to convince my players that Yorkshire and the others could be beaten.'

So in his own, often dogmatic, way - to reactions from the old pros that ranged sharply from glum disapproval and perhaps discreet scepticism to grudging acquiescence - he forged a tough, incestuous team spirit. In the wider world of county cricket, where murmurs of anti-Welsh bigotry could still be detected, the Wooller methods were not always universally acclaimed. 'He's making 'em too bleeding combative and aggressive,' others would say. He saw that as a compliment; it was the sort of 'accolade' once reserved only for Yorkshire and the North Country elite.

Under him in 1948, Glamorgan won the Championship with, if not the best side in the table, then certainly the most wholehearted and highly disciplined one. 'We caught everything above the ground,' he assured me. He'd always seen fielding as a prerequisite of success. His intrepid leg-side fields brought a new fashion to county cricket. The forward, square and backward short legs seemed to hold on to everything, without flinching. Wooller led by example in the forward position, wearing the bruises like a Pontypool prop's battle-scars. In some respects, he never spiritually divided the two games. They were both physical, quite apart from the additional subtleties of cricket that he readily acknowledged; both were about courage and stuffing the opposition.

His gamesmanship was notorious. He made no attempt to excuse it; he saw nothing wrong with it. The stage whispers he exchanged with his wicket-keeper paled many a timorous opposing batsman. The Wooller observation could also be caustic. During that rather soured match at Trent Bridge, when an exasperated Simpson dared to bowl underarm to the Glamorgan skipper, Wilf in turn offered one or two variants from the norm when it was Nottinghamshire's time to bat. He bowled slowish in-swingers to a field which, apart from a third man and cover, was exclusively on the leg side. 'I got Reg caught at short leg to one of my deliveries that dipped late. And that caused Charlie Harris, at the other end, to start blocking everything.

'In a loud voice I said that I really *thought* those blokes from Nottinghamshire could *hit* the ball . . . You could sense the atmosphere after that. They got themselves out and I made them follow-on. It was eventually a draw but my remark had had its effect on their batting.'

Wooller talks without an iota of shame of what he calls legitimate gamesmanship. He argues that it is part of the game, and would scoff at the merest implication that it verges on cheating.

'Here, let me tell you what I consider is fair. In a match a ball suddenly lifts to the obvious surprise of the batsman. I go down the wicket and say to a fielder, in a voice which can be heard by the batsman, that I think the wicket is breaking up. The seed has then been sown.' There is a sparkle in his eye as he cites this so-called hypothetical case. You know, and he knows you know, that he had plucked it straight from his own treasure chest of contentious memories.

He *was* Glamorgan cricket. He captained them from 1947-60 and was secretary for thirty-one fruitful if never too sedate years until 1978. Now he's the president. As a player he achieved the double in 1954. His 13,600 runs at 22.57 contained five hundreds, one of them against the West Indies just before the war. He took 958 wickets at 26.96; he could swing the ball both ways. The physique reflected the stamina, never more tested than when Hammond scored the second of his triple hundreds against Glamorgan, this time at Newport in 1939. 'It was a quite magnificent innings,' says the bowler, who must have been wondering at the time whether this was quite the most productive way to spend a fortnight's summer holiday.

While still at Rydal, his allegiance geographically at least leaned towards Lancashire. He actually had a few matches for Lancashire 2nd X1 while at school. But he came south and had five games for Glamorgan in 1938.

Maybe his exceptional merits as a captain were at times obscured by the volume of the invective. But at this distance we can see more clearly his qualities. It wasn't simply his rugged leadership. He possessed a rare intuition, allied to a personal knowledge of the techniques, and flaws, of the majority of the batsmen he was going to come up against. He studiously set a specific field for every one of his bowlers. And the rest he left to safe, almost infallible, hands.

He wasn't in any sense a privileged amateur. There wasn't enough money to bring up a family along with the indulgences of going on tour. Arlott always believed Wooller would have been an outstanding captain of England. He was, in fact, invited to go as vice-captain under George Mann to South Africa in 1948-49. Then there was a strong lobby for him to lead his country on the cricket tour of India in 1951-52, and he was asked if he'd be available. He was never an egotist. Practicalities of domestic life outweighed the glory and he shook his head.

—

Wooller did, of course, captain Wales at rugby. After reluctantly giving up soccer, he'd started to play in the pack at school. 'You're too fast to be a forward,' his headmaster told him. 'Learn how to pass the ball.' And that was how he became such an exhilarating centre, though he did appear against the All Blacks on the wing. He played at Twickenham when Wales beat England there for the first time. His drop-goals and kicking generally were prodigious. Some of the kicks are still talked about, part of rugby folklore in the Valleys. His running with the ball was distinctive and, for those poised to tackle him, quite frightening. He attacked with teeth clenched and knees pumping high.

'I played flat out.' It's his favourite way of telling you how he played, whether at rugby or cricket. 'When the game was over, that was it. Absolutely no aggro. So different now.' But does distance not lend a tinge or two of romance? In the clubhouse at Neath not so many years ago, I eavesdropped on a scrumful of ancient pundits engaged in timeless evaluation. 'That Wilf Wooller could drop one over from his own half. But he was a hard bugger. Just as likely to break your jaw when you went to tackle him, with his high menacing knees going like those of a runaway thoroughbred.' Mixed metaphors, maybe - but those shared, hairy memories down at the Gnoll couldn't have been more graphic.

Wilfred Wooller, from craggy and ever-bracing Rhos-on-Sea, was and is quintessentially a spartan. He really belonged to the open air: where you could sniff the salty tang of the foaming waves or the sweat of a marauding pack. His men were strong and brave. They cussed and didn't concede ground. They licked their wounds and didn't belly-ache. He baled them out in private, defended them from misplaced acrimony in public. The rugby or the cricket pitch were no places for sentiment; he reserved those feelings for the family he loved. When Roger Davis was seriously injured during a match and nearly died, Wooller was to say to Tony Lewis: 'It's like war. Someone goes down and you've got to get someone else in there straightaway. Crying about Roger is going to make you a bad side.' Lewis, the gentle violinist, a more sensitive and emotional Welshman, saw again the worldly soldier who had experienced too much of man's inhumanity to man in the Far East.

Lewis was in many ways his pupil, the grammar schoolboy he had groomed for the Glamorgan captaincy and who was there when the county, with their finest side, won the title in 1969. Lewis, at first hand, observed the contrasting qualities - half at least of them, it would appear, endearing.

In his autobiography, Tony Lewis pinpoints the Saturday night when he felt Wilf had accepted him 'as a worthy amateur tough enough to play first-class cricket'. It was a convivial gathering in a Nottingham hotel, where the Glamorgan team were celebrating with, and drinking their generous share of, a crate of champagne awarded to Peter Walker for his recent tally of catches. Suddenly, without the merest warning, the skipper grabbed an ornate and no doubt expensive clock from the lounge mantelpiece and hurled it, in the style of a scrum-half, towards Lewis at the other end of the room. The clock was so heavy, the power in the wrist and forearms of the thrower so immense, that the startled Neath fullback was thrown back into the fireplace. His rib cage suffered a stabbing pain but he held onto the catch. What was more, he returned the weighty clock in similar fashion. Wilf nonchalantly 'plucked it out of the air and returned it to the shelf'. The team applauded the wanton charade.

The young amateur must have feared he'd cracked half a dozen ribs. He went to the lavatory as discreetly as possible and discovered that he was being followed.

'Bloody great. You got up and threw it back. Now they know what you're made of,' said Wooller.

There must have been something about seasoned cricketers and reckless physical feats on a Saturday evening when the day's play was done. Somerset had a pre-war New Zealand amateur, Tom Lowry, who captained both Cambridge and his country. He liked to demonstrate his sheer strength while the ale was flowing. His speciality, to the accompaniment of sustained applause, was single-handedly to transport solid pieces of furniture - like hotel pianos - from the foyer to first floor landings. It was an eternal riddle to the early-morning staff.

But surely there was no bigger riddle than Wooller himself. Few post-war cricketing figures have aroused such contrasting passions. Maurice Turnbull, who like him was a double blue at Cambridge and played international rugby and squash for Wales, was his mentor. Wooller watched and admired the no-nonsense approach, the manner in which responsibilities were accepted and decisions made without reservation. That became, only more so, the Wooller style. He carried it out with a bellicose voice and size twelve boots.

When last we chatted, he was as opinionated as ever. There were still commies under the bed. He was as witheringly intolerant as ever with do-gooders, as he saw them in that quaintly *passé* way. Intolerant of many aspects of modern life, in fact. Making sure I didn't for a moment get the impression that he was in danger of going soft in old age. But then he came back to his bowls again. 'Such a *friendly* game, you know. That's what appeals to me.'

So your critics got you hopelessly wrong after all. You old, confusing charmer. Bloody Wilf Wooller . . .

TWO

SIEGFRIED SASSOON

Inner Peace at Mid-on

———

Sassoon, Siegfried Louvain. Born Weirleigh, Kent,
1886. Died Heytesbury, Wiltshire, 1967.
English poet, best known for his savagely satirical
poems exposing the horrors of war, based on his
experiences in the trenches 1914-18. Wounded in
action twice, awarded the MC, then became a pacifist.
Also known for his three-volume fictional
autobiography, Memoirs of a Fox-Hunting Man, etc,
with its loving evocation of country pursuits. A village
cricketer of indeterminate talent.

SIEGFRIED SASSOON'S ALMOST comically gawky physique and saturnine features should be discounted. He was perhaps at his happiest of all on the cricket field. The childhood innocence, scarred through as it was by the horrors of the trenches and other private torments, was still discernible as he stationed himself at mid-on to miss his catches and think again of Woolley, his imperishable hero.

Sassoon's cricket, mildly better in his own Kentish days with Bluemantles than when he ambled across the parkland from Heytesbury House, in Wiltshire, to play alongside his estate workers, a few local farmers and boys from the village, was languidly enthusiastic. It was also, whatever he may occasionally have believed in his romantic flights, undistinguished.

Tucked discreetly into the late middle-order, he demonstrated an upright stance and an apparent propensity for the off drive. The stroke carried something of a flourish, lingering on from the stereotyped tuition of his schooldays. His most charitable intimates would not imply it was handsomely executed. There was evidence that he attempted, rather ambitiously, to add the late cut to his quirky and restricted repertoire. It seems to have been no more than a grandiose gesture, alien to the practicalities in hand, to parade suddenly on a sunny day.

His amiable teammates, not least those who worked for him, did their best to see him into double figures. There was from everyone an obsessive determination not to run him out, though he was known to turn up unexpectedly without invitation at his partner's end. Such aberrations called for a shrug of resignation and saintly self-sacrifice on some bewildered parishioner's part.

Erstwhile partners to whom I spoke described his batting variously as quaint, eccentric, limited and very ordinary. 'Very ordinary' was an evaluation offered without a semblance of malice or even denigration. Dennis Silk, until quite recently the respected and perspicacious Warden at Radley College and a former

—

Somerset cricketer, who knew him well, contemplated Siegfried's aggregate of skills and range of shots, and suggested that he might end up with an average of 17 in a good season. One suspects that friendship lent generosity to the calculation.

Sassoon liked it best of all in the nets. Here he could thrust forward his left foot in the classic tradition and pretend he was a Kent pro, or even one of those ostentatious amateurs from Tunbridge Wells or Canterbury flashing wanton cover boundaries while on leave from the colonial service. He liked the relaxation of the nets. There were no tiresome exertions. Sometimes he'd come out of the Big House at Heytesbury, after a morning in bed reading the papers. He always began with *The Times* - and the cricket scores. They were apt to stir his angular, indolent frame.

'I say, Gearing. Where are young Reynolds and Kitley? I'd like them to bowl at me for half an hour in the nets.'

Bill Gearing was the head gardener. He would stifle an oath, less than pleased at the prospect of losing two able-bodied workers. But at Heytesbury House life was kept in perspective, however confusing that sometimes appeared to the staff. If Henry Reynolds and Jim Kitley were needed to roll up their sleeves and pitch half volleys of obliging pace and direction, rather than hack out the weeds between the onion rows, then so be it. They had no complaints as they pounded up in their hobnails.

When Edmund Blunden, Sassoon's friend for forty years or so, stayed at Heytesbury he was taken to watch him in the nets at Downside. Those were the days when Sassoon also played for the Ravens, a worthy and esoteric team with a formidable membership, emanating from the enthusiasms of the Benedictine community there and especially those of the founder, Dom Aidan Trafford. All the Ravens' home matches were played on the delightful School ground during the holidays.

Sassoon was essentially an introspective man, who saved his

—

talking - whether on theology or the war - for long, nocturnal sessions in the library after dinner. But suddenly, quite out of character, he'd become impish in the nets, and balance a shilling on the stumps in an act of bravado and challenge to the bowlers.

Claims by one or two of his literary friends that he was still turning up in his cream flannels, two or three inches too short for him just like the trousers he wore, when he was into his eighties are a nice but inaccurate notion. One of his last matches for the Ravens was against Ronald Knox's and Christopher Hollis's Mells. Sassoon was about seventy-eight and had announced he was thinking of giving up the great game. The Ravens, in the managerial hands of Father Martin, a housemaster at Downside, were both talented and unconventional in matter of batting order. They still played hard and made great efforts to win in the evening shadows or last over: as a concession perhaps to the local brewery trade. Ideally the opposition batted first; the aim was to leave the Ravens with a total to stretch or even inspire them after tea.

The club had a prepossessing skill in stage-management. They would, with an amalgam of cunning and good nature, embrace the confidence of the opposition. The ecclesiastical captain had a persuasive manner. And when it came to the fixture with Mells, there was a corporate ploy of stealth to give Siegfried a valedictory lift towards the elusive double figures. Mells introduced an excessively slow bowler of negligible merit. The ancient batsman played the first four deliveries with wary correctness. He tried to hit the next for six, rather grandly, back over the bowler - and gave mid-on an embarrassingly easy catch.

Sassoon snorted to himself and proclaimed to no one specifically as he came in: 'The bowling was not worthy of me.'

That was his batting. His bowling, essayed in schooldays, wasn't risked at club level. It was his fielding that generated most comment and amusement, mostly out of earshot. Father Martin described it as 'appalling but of immense courage'. He knew only too well Sassoon's lack of mobility and was inclined to act as his runner when batting for Ravens. 'I couldn't trust anyone else - for fear of a mistake.' Could anything be more evocative than this metaphor of Sassoon playing cricket: 'One of those old gramophones with horns, a little cracked . . . you felt there had been something there at one time.' It was said with much affection.

His absence of coordination in the field, increasingly evident in his last few years with Heytesbury and the Ravens, was as engaging as it was hypnotic. Two of his contemporaries recalled his bird-like appearance. Dennis Silk saw him like a wading-bird, picking his legs up high as he walked. Another old friend specified the crane before switching his ornithological image to the heron. 'I was influenced by that disproportionately large and long head and those angular movements.'

He positioned himself as of right at mid-on, a gaunt, statuesque figure. When the batsman struck the ball firmly in his direction Siegfried remained stiffly to attention, allowing it to crack against his unprotected shins. The rest of the team would wince and do their best to suppress gentle guffaws. He would then, in very much his own time, stoop to pick up the ball and return it underarm to the bowler.

The immobility could be taken to extremes. On his own ground at Heytesbury, he held the unspoken feudal authority without the nominal captaincy. His staff cut the outfield and kept the square manicured, and laden with runs. The club had the facilities for nothing. In return he was allowed to field where he wished - and to go more or less anywhere he chose in the batting order. Sometimes on a whim he went in relatively early to partner Sam Dredge, the Downs shepherd whose pastoral philosophy he shared. Sassoon could perhaps articulate it rather better, but they both had a profound distrust of intellectuals. 'The Captain' was usually put, with some tact, at No 7, 8 or 9. This met with his tacit approval. No one ever dared to drop the squire to last man.

His Heytesbury teammates despaired of his catching ability. He would post himself in the dreamy hinterland of the leg side, and on hot Saturday afternoons meander deep into the outfield on occasions. His rambles were accepted. Logic and the state of the game didn't come into it. Roy Newman, later to be the skipper of the village side, played only a few matches alongside him. He was astonished to see him desert the outfield altogether at times, to sit on the iron fence or lean against the gate.

Once when playing for the Ravens on a cold day, he had cussedly kept his hands in his pockets when offered the easiest of catches. In explanation to no one in particular, he said: 'If I'd tried to catch that one, I'm sure I should have strained something.'

This is no more than a warm-hearted vignette of Sassoon as a makeshift club cricketer. But to know him, the most underrated writer of our time in the view of Silk, just a little better, it is valuable to reflect on the game that ran like a stabilising thread through his complex life. He watched country house and village cricket during his privileged upbringing in Kent. In Victorian England he played on the lawn with his less enthusiastic brothers and Mr Moon, his private tutor. He played his first game on Matfield Green when he was still a boy, scoring eight of the team's total of 13. He squeezed into the house team at school and later spent hours at Fenner's, when he found law at Cambridge 'too inhuman and arid'. He bought the evening paper to see the stop press scores.

School life wasn't always agreeable. 'Onion' was hardly the most complimentary of nicknames. He found Marlborough 'moderately pleasant but mentally unprofitable'. His father had left home when Siegfried was seven and that drew him tightly to the bosom of his artistic mother. He was always inclined to be introverted: and

—

cricket was the perfect outlet for the solitary boy and man who still wanted people around him.

It wasn't the same following the hounds in the guise of George Sherston. There was too much noise: their yelps and blood-scented barks, the crescendo of horses' hooves, the incessant bonhomie of the gentry in their hunting livery, flush-faced and stirrup-breathed. Cricket, by contrast, embraced in its quiet all the byways of the imagination. If you were Sassoon, you sat for an hour, pads on and yellowing bat on your lap, waiting your turn and needing to talk. And you could dream when you went out to field - of when the majestic Woolley mended a puncture for you (as he did once for the idolising Siegfried) or played the first of his Tests for England before the First World War.

At cricket you could drift from the game and still be part of it. Surrounded by ten other fielders. Sassoon could look up above Heytesbury House at the dense, timeless woodland that he loved and needed. He knew every ash and beech tree and, if requested, would take his house guests to the trunk of the only oak on the estate. Whenever he walked the woods, he made sure the secateurs were in his jacket pocket. When, twenty years ago, I did the research for a television documentary on the great, often misunderstood poet, his son George told me of the hours Siegfried spent, utterly contented in his chosen solitude, cutting back the bracken.

'Catch it, Captain Sassoon,' would snap him, invariably too late, from his reveries. The 'Oh, bloody hell' from a momentarily exasperated bowler was less audible. His remoteness was accepted. Who was to know whether Mad Jack's darker thoughts of the trench carnage, the loss of dear friends, the wounds and the shell-shocked confusion, and all the self doubts that clouded his domestic life, remained agonisingly close, ever liable to return and haunt him, whether he was on horseback, in the library or out on the cricket field?

—

It is quite certain that cricket was a soothing therapy. That serious, still handsome face would break into a look of pure innocent joy when a well-heeled braggart from a neighbouring parish was bowled. He enjoyed the teas at the Angel Inn, this shy man who couldn't talk easily with his workers playing for him but who would sit enthralled, listening to their teatime tales of village life.

When he wrote *The Old Century* in 1936-37, it was above all a simple, domestic chronicle of innocence, 'a happy dream which relieved my troubled mind.' There was a rather beautiful naïvety about 'my simple minded belief that the world was full of extremely nice people if only one could get to know them properly . . .'

He liked, almost without exception, the nice people with whom he played cricket. Here, in a way, was his idealism: the kind that caused him to flirt briefly with socialism and to work for the *Daily Herald*. A cricket team was a microcosm of disparate people, blending in peace and good nature amid the tranquillity of the countryside. He overlooked the fact that he could relate so much more naturally to other landowners and the schoolmasters at Downside than to the under-gardeners on the estate. One should blame not him but the rigid class structure and the inhibitions caused by his kind of leisured background, for that.

Sassoon had grown up to believe that the staff should play cricket. Richardson, an early groom, was very good indeed and should, according to the master, have played for Kent. Successive tutors earned his eternal respect if they could pitch on a length in the back garden.

His work force at Heytesbury House was also, one suspects, recruited with an eye to their potential prowess on a Saturday afternoon. The house itself, large rather than attractive, was on the site of a medieval mansion and carried more than a whiff of high drama. Walter, Lord Hungerford, was stopped in his tracks when

—

engaged on enlarging the building. He was arrested, charged with treason and beheaded. Henry V111 seized the whole property. For years it remained semi-derelict. Sassoon was married in 1932; he came to Heytesbury, and stayed till his death in 1967.

When he arrived, Heytesbury was a quiet, isolated village. It was quite an occasion for the parishioners to go the four miles into Warminster. Sassoon loved the sylvan hillsides and decided the new home was conducive to poetry-writing and all those copious entries in his diary. He ensured that the surrounds of the house and the whole grounds were kept immaculate. For that purpose he engaged five men to work in the woods and five more in the gardens. In addition, there were two to look after the stables and the cars - and a staff of eight indoors.

The cricket pitch was tended by his workers. It was much envied 'and everyone wanted to play on it'. The square was almost up to county standard. Captain Sassoon would stroll down to supervise the rolling. 'He was a nice man and it was a treat to work there. The only trouble was that he didn't pay very well.' The Big House never did in those days.

Five of his men played for the team. Old Bill Gearing, the head gardener, was captain. Bert Turner, who as second gardener looked after the greenhouses, was the wicket-keeper. Ernie Stancer, who doubled up as groom and chauffeur, had the build of a jockey which helped when he raced round the boundary. And then 'the young garden boys', Henry Reynolds and Jim Kitley, used to open the bowling. Jim was slightly faster and was allowed to bowl down the hill.

Sassoon liked to involve himself in team selection. It wasn't wholly democratic. But there was always a place for his five strong-muscled workers, who did their best to disguise their eagerness when they learned of a Wednesday fixture. The wages may have been poor but there was time off without question when it came to

—

an important mid-week match.

Sam Dredge, Sam the Shepherd, was a favourite of Siegfried's. He was a gentle countryman who opened the innings and had been known to score a hundred with the air of serenity you would expect from a man of the Wiltshire Downs. It seemed equally appropriate that Sam should be the club's spin bowler. As for the Heytesbury farmers who found a place in the village eleven, they were mostly burly of shoulders and thighs, and healthily red of face. One of them, Johnny Perrott, braced himself for massive sixes in a way that caused the poetic chairman of selectors to chuckle and ponder a shaft of romantic imagery.

For away matches and the occasional journey to Warminster, he drove his two-seater Humber. He drove it badly, though no doubt oblivious to the consternation caused to successive passengers and other road users. He wasn't adept at reading the highway signs and assumed a seemingly autocratic, but in truth absent-minded, regard towards right of way. He had the vehicle specially built for his wife in the days when there was still a marital affinity. One companion of his would see the car chugging uneasily into view, and then summon up all the eloquence necessary with a plaintive shake of the head. 'It was too tacky for words. There were yellow joins on the outside to keep the water out.'

Sassoon, after his war poems and the new creative dimension to his work, had become for a time a fashionable figure in literary circles and, certainly by Wiltshire standards, quite a celebrity. Visiting teams would look towards him in awe during the tea intervals at the Angel. Some of them had got hold of the Mad Jack tag and speculated on what he might do if a teammate ran him out.

The villagers didn't see much of him apart from home matches. His lifestyle intrigued them. 'He do stay in bed half the day — and writes them poems all through the night' . . . 'He's a bit of a rummun. Leaves the phone ringing, never answers it. His friends get quite annoyed' . . . 'He loves playing the piano, you know' . . . 'In a dream much of the time, he is. Wanders past you without seeing you at all' . . .

But they all knew he was special. They weren't too sure of the details, though they had heard in a vague way of his immense courage as a soldier. Some were convinced he'd won the VC. It was an understandable mistake as he had been recommended for the ultimate award for bravery. 'Captain Sassoon got the MC,' they were told by those with the more reliable memories. 'And he chucked it away.'

No one was quite certain why. As this diffident man walked out with his under-gardeners, groom and a few farmers, after losing the toss in mid-July, it was quite impossible to associate him with the valour of a Welch Guards officer who brought back a wounded lance-corporal under heavy fire, and who later captured a German trench single-handed.

He hated the publicity that followed, and persisted on and off for the rest of his life. Fleet Street once let him down and he never forgave. When journalists asked if they could call, he said no. If they wanted to talk with him about the war and his poetry, he'd cut them short with a dismissive: 'I'm only prepared to have a word with you about cricket.' That was the last thing they wanted.

The cult of celebrity embarrassed him. Dennis Silk told me: 'It was different if he was in the presence of a great cricketer. There was a boyish excitement about him then - he was totally unaware of his own greatness.'

He loved to be in the company of cricketers. He turned up at Fenner's in 1953 and self-consciously introduced himself to Silk.

'I remember clearly the gaunt, handsome stranger in moth-eaten blue blazer and faded trilby hat, who marched up to the pavilion with a long forked hazel staff in his hand,' Silk was to recall in a Guinness Lecture at the Salisbury Festival of the Arts.

—

Much later he was to tell me: 'Siegfried watched us playing and then took us all to the Garden House Hotel for a slap-up dinner. He entertained us to a virtuoso performance on cricketers' initials. He had a wonderful memory, especially for the initials of Kent players before the First World War.'

In the Cambridge party was the turbaned Sikh, Swaranjit Singh, who was twelfth man in 1954 and won his blue the following summer. A nervous waiter, possibly distracted by the strange drift of Sassoon's unabated monologue, stumbled and deposited a whole bowl of soup on poor Singh.

'Oh, Christ,' someone said.

Siegfried had been in full flow. His mood was jocular. 'Let me see, now. Christ J. was it?'

He puffed on his pipe and everyone laughed. A moment of abject embarrassment had passed.

The friendship between Sassoon and Silk grew. It is easy to see why. The Warden of Radley - as he was until his fairly recent retirement and return to the old cricketing pastures of Somerset - is himself a gentle, rounded, civilised man, a scholar without ostentation, literate, a lover of poetry and someone with a similar sense of quiet fun. And in those sunny undergraduate days he was also, to the transparent delight of Sassoon, a cricketer. He got his blue three years running for Cambridge; he went on to play thirty-three times for Somerset. His county teammates liked him and said he batted with the conscientious efficiency of a pro. At short leg he took all the catches that came his way. He was a big success when he captained the MCC teams in North America and New Zealand. Like Siegfried, he combined the sensitivity of the bookish man with a physical aptitude. When it came to outdoor competitiveness, Silk was rather better, of course. He also played for Cambridge and Sussex at rugby. It was much admired by his mentor.

Dennis Silk was still a student, a learner, a listener in the early days of their friendship. He was invited down to Heytesbury in the August. They talked the night away, or rather Sassoon did. 'My role was to be a listener, he was still haunted by World War One and he called himself the Hermit of Heytesbury.' The ghastly gunfire rumbled on as they sat, the tormented talker and the transfixed listener, until the light of dawn came through the library windows.

> I see them in foul dug-outs, gnawed by rats
> And in the ruined trenches lashed with rain.
> Dreaming of things they did with balls and bat
> And mocked by hopeless longing to regain
> Bank-holidays, and picture shows, and spats,
> And going to the office in the train . . .

He needed, even in the mid-Fifties, to go on talking about it as part of the long, painful process of purging the experiences from his system. Occasionally, as in that extract from the poem 'Dreamers', he would interweave cricketing imagery with that of the Somme. Those evenings at Heytesbury were a life's education for Silk. As a historian he chose Marlborough after leaving Cambridge. The proximity to Heytesbury thrilled Sassoon, who even bought the young schoolmaster an old Austin 10 to make the visits easier.

They played together for the Ravens. This somewhat arcane club, formed in 1921 and relaunched with typical zest by Father Martin, himself a brave sailor-turned Benedictine monk, in 1951, had a haphazard but distinguished membership. Ben Barnett, the Australian wicket-keeper, played a game or two. Jack Fingleton, a good friend, only umpired. Tony Pearson, stirringly remembered for the way he took all ten wickets against Leicestershire at Loughborough when playing for Cambridge, was another Raven,

—

no doubt because of his links with Downside. The Roebuck brothers, Peter and Paul, also played - as did the affable Somerset amateur, Hugh Watts. At the latest count, they could boast over the variegated years one English Test player, eleven county cricketers, a dozen blues and at least four members of Minor Counties status.

It was a club of flawless ecumenical intent, even if the matches were played on the Catholic college ground. Sassoon, who was received into the Roman Catholic faith, there at Downside Abbey in 1957, airily stood his ground at mid-on. Jock Henderson, the Bishop of Bath and Wells, was steadfastly rooted to the lush pastures of mid-off. They exchanged cricketing rather than theological badinage, and left more fleet-footed Ravens to cover for their physical ineptitude. It was a chummy club of sharply varying talents. The chances of selection helped if you were a friend of the skipper. John Luff, a quarry owner on the Mendips, was one. He never quite got over running out his brother on 99. John made his runs for the Ravens before transporting himself in the spirit of collective immobility to first slip for the rest of the match, either very fine or very wide at the behest of his Benedictine better.

As a club it could be as eccentric as Sassoon himself. There was an element of seriousness about one or two of the members. They were less than enchanted when I once referred to them publicly as oddball. With a misplaced solemnity, they suggested I gave too much of an impression of convivial rural incompetence. I can only report that the Ravens didn't, as far as I could ascertain, have too many rules - if any at all. No one was scolded if a dolly was missed while the fielder was abstractedly admiring the delicate folds of the surrounding countryside.

Cricket as an institution and ritual was important to Sassoon, just as the hunting pink had been. Yet the feudal side of his interest was only nominal, a concession to his background. The war had made him more liberal and he privately wished he could have shown it more as he sat in front of the old pavilion, waiting his turn to bat. He loved the shepherd and the chirpy village boys, especially when they bowled out the opposition by four o'clock. Sadly his classlessness remained theoretical.

Cricket was his game because it gave him space and time. If his eyes misted over as he reflected again on how his best friend died from a rifle bullet, no one knew. Mid-on was as good a cavern as anywhere for introspection: offering as much solitude as he found on his daily stroll through the woodland of his estate. There were times when he needed to unburden himself, to wreak his anger on man's inhumanity: it helped when Edmund Blunden was around to share and do his best to absorb some of the pain, before lightening the gloom with a droll memory of Fenner's.

By the time I went to Heytesbury House, up the long winding gravel drive to research and ponder the life of the late master for that television programme, the flowers, once so profuse, were drooping and less fussed over. The parkland cricket pitch wasn't quite so immaculate. In a few years' time there would be a noisy, intrusive bypass, to cut off the House entirely from the pitch. Whatever would Captain Sassoon have said?

The village team, nowadays without the estate workers, still takes on the neighbouring parishes. The older players still talk affectionately of Siegfried and suspect he'd approve of the consistent artisan skills and playing record. Son George is the president and comes to watch the occasional match. Kindly, apocryphal stories about The Captain, of permanently bruised shins and lamentable fielding, are resurrected every Saturday summer's evening in the two local pubs.

He was 'an English country gentleman to his bones, the echo of a bygone age'. Those who remember him, and the rest of us who pretend we do, see still that mesmeric Edwardian figure: awkward in stature, a decent and good man, a shy, troubled, doubting, complex one.

Sassoon needed his loneliness. The loneliness he cherished most of all was in the crowded, silent company of his timeless trees; in the company of the nuns and the monks who could communicate without conversation; and, maybe above all, amid the sublime innocence of a freshly mown outfield.

THREE

JACK FINGLETON

Radical with a Taste for Toffs

Fingleton, John Henry Webb.
Born Waverley, New South Wales,
Australia 1908.
Died Sydney 1981. Opening bat.
New South Wales (1928-29 to
1939-40, 49 matches).
Tests: 18. Tours to South Africa
1935-36 and England 1938.
Distinguished political and cricket
journalist and author.

THERE IS, I ACCEPT, SOMETHING far too presumptuous in writing at length about an Australian cricketer and writer I never watched and one I met, in the most peripheral sense, no more than three times.

Jack Fingleton had come here on a single tour as a player, in 1938. My knowledge then as a schoolboy of his technical skills was minimal. He struck me, from the newspaper reports I read so avidly, as a pretty dour batsman - obscured by the prodigious shadows cast by the Don and, rather less so, Stan McCabe. I couldn't remember the 1932-33 furore, but everyone told me Fingleton was as brave as anyone in the Australian team at the time the predestined missiles reared wickedly towards the rib-cage or head.

Then, long after, I met him in the press box at Taunton and Bristol. In truth, I didn't really talk to him; more accurately, I eavesdropped, chuckled to myself, and savoured my good fortune in being in such company. Not that there was much room to talk, let alone work, in the poky, Dickensian box at Taunton, where John Arlott coveted the Bob Cratchit inkwells, and you arrived early in pursuit of a reasonable vantage point.

Somehow Fingleton and his impish fellow Irishman, Lindsay Hassett, defied the strictures of claustrophobia. They both had plenty to say. In Hassett's case, the words were eternally ebullient; in Fingleton's, barbed, a trifle cynical, but also mirthful.

They sparked off each other. Fingo's observations on the match in progress were unfailingly perceptive. I mentally filed the occasional phrase to plagiarise, no doubt, in some future report for my beloved and long lamented *Bristol Evening World*.

Hassett and Fingleton were foils for each other. The Fingleton rejoiner could be vastly entertaining. But his mood was the more tetchy. He was impatient with facetious remarks, of which there are many over the day in an incestuous press box of general bonhomie.

—

54

I used to idolise my elders as they pontificated or penned their prose. They weren't always as I expected them to be. People would talk of Robertson-Glasgow's gregarious nature; at Glastonbury, where the wind used to whistle down from the Tor on an early-season Saturday, he huddled silently in the back of the Festival tent. He was refreshingly courteous when he came to borrow my office phone for his tea-time report to *The Observer*. For most of the time this thoroughly nice man appeared preoccupied. The demons may already have been gnawing inside his head. Life became unbearable for him not long afterwards.

But you invariably knew of Fingleton's presence. The waspish tongue, which could be so amusing, wasn't exactly uncommon among the Australian players and reporters. I put it down at the time, with a judgment that was perhaps a trifle too facile, to the supposed deep-seated Antipodean complexes. With my scant knowledge of Aussie history, encompassing imperialistic heavy-handedness and malpractice, I reckoned I could understand the reason for the weighty shoulder chips and the way many Australians reacted with a defensive swagger.

Fingo never pussyfooted in his life. His views, on almost any subject, were unequivocal. The gutless indulgence of sitting on the fence passed him by. If there was a cricketer or a politician he didn't like, he said so. At the same time he could be petulant and unduly sensitive over personal criticism. Quite apart from offering a withering rebuke in a letter to someone he felt had offended him, he was known to fire off a few writs, more to frighten than penalise in the pocket.

He had no time at all for fast bowlers who took all day to bowl their overs, or who kept pitching the ball short with vicious intent - nor for the captains who encouraged it. He was as critical of the Australians as of the West Indians. It was possible to make a long list, detectable from the way he wrote his reports, of the players for

—

whom he had no affectionate regard. Boycott would have come in that category. 'He's a good Test batsman, of course, but the most selfish cricketer I have ever known.' One particularly trenchant article about Boycott in *The Sunday Times* upset many of the Yorkshire loyalists.

His attitude towards fellow occupants of the Aussie dressing-room, of which more later, varied acutely. A contemporary broadcaster, Alan McGilvray, with whom he once indiscreetly argued a cricketing point when the mike was still live, was probably not a favourite dinner companion. He had an ambivalent relationship with John Arlott and claimed in print that the much-esteemed Burr of Basingstoke wouldn't broadcast with him. 'But you do take the piss out of me,' Arlott is supposed to have said to him in one evening of shared confidences. It was possibly true.

And did Fingo not like Sir Hugh Carleton Green? There was certainly unmitigated venom in the way he once laid into him. Fingleton could be, whatever his radical roots, a man of fiercely reactionary views. He despised many of society's new-fangled ideas, on and off the field. He had no time at all 'for queers and Commies'.

So, in his privileged role as interviewer, he was ready to take on the poor, unsuspecting Sir Hugh, who thought he was on a nice, bland visit to Canberra as Director-General of the BBC. The broad-shouldered emissary had been imprudent enough to make it known he never shied away from tough questions. 'Right, my old Pommie,' thought Fingleton, adept in the ways and methods of newspapers. He was already thinking in terms of cabled headlines and ruffled feathers.

'Well, yes,' spluttered Sir Hugh, there were probably what Fingleton chose to call 'queers and Commies' in the Corporation. But that was surely inevitable in any big organisation, after all. The opportunistic interviewer got the response he secretly wanted.

Afterwards, Sir Hugh told his entourage that he was pretty shocked by the line of questioning. When next in England himself, Fingo was to tell friends he imagined that particular interview, liberally displayed by *The Sunday Times* (after their lawyers had taken a wary look at it and the author had been asked more than once whether he was absolutely sure about his quotes), had perhaps seriously jeopardised his prospects of regular future work for the BBC.

'Family life is so important,' he would say recurrently in explanation of what he admitted was a somewhat pejorative attitude towards homosexuals.

There was much of contradiction about Fingleton. Despite some views that smacked of intractable bigotry - not on racial matters, it should be said - he could be a most kind and compassionate person. As so many will tell you, he helped to settle Harold Larwood in Australia. He was inordinately generous when he stayed with friends in England: he took good wine with him on arrival and would leave expensive jewellery for the hostess when he left.

He admitted he enjoyed the company of 'a few of the English toffs' but was vocally proud of his proletarian roots back in Sydney, and the fact that the mother he idolised somehow managed, with not many material comforts, to bring up five children. To one Catholic priest, whom he trusted implicitly, he said he valued above all things a secure family unit. Yet, in its fullest sense, it eluded him. The strained, at times frigid, state of his own marriage was a strange and ironic commentary on a man who held such an idealised attitude towards marital co-existence. It left him miserable at times; it crept repeatedly into his conversation.

The three sons and two daughters meant much to him. His wife, Philippa, earned no more than one cursory mention in his autobiography. Their lifestyles and outlooks were different. One good and lasting friend of Fingo told me: 'There was a permanent tug in his life - between his work as a writer, taking him often away from home, and being with his family. I honestly believe he'd have given up his cricket altogether if he could have saved his marriage. That at least was his retrospective feeling'. Signs of a reconciliation were detected by some towards the end.

Fingleton could be intensely private. He went his own way professionally. As a political journalist, he found his own stories and shuffled off to type them. On tour as a cricket writer, he spent more time than most in his own hotel room. Sometimes his daughter Belinda, known as 'Bin', an attractive, fun-loving girl, would come to England with him. 'I wish Philippa had been more interested in cricket,' he would say.

He knew that cricket, at the international level at least, and marriage simply didn't mix. One or two of the players, at one time, would give 'Bin' the kind of glance which suggested their minds were not wholly on the match in progress. McKenzie was among those thought to fancy her. Fingo was proud of her. 'Whatever you do, don't marry a cricketer,' he used to say with a smile, but from the depths of bitter experience.

In the moments of solitude that he intermittently seemed to need, he pondered too obsessively on the past. He harboured grievances in the grand manner. He thought - and wouldn't let go mentally - of Bradman. The rancour became part of Australian cricketing folklore.

There had been too many slights in his sporting life and he had every right to remember them, he would tell well-meaning companions who advised him it was time to forget. 'Time to forget the petty whim of logic that kept me out of the 1934 tour of England?' he would ask. He was a modest man and didn't need to add that the omission came so soon after the legendary courage he'd shown against Larwood and Voce.

But he would say, a defiant timbre to the voice: 'Was it because of the Lie?' Just that.

There was a general conviction, especially among cricket's establishment, that Fingleton was to blame for the infamous leak of dressing-room information during the Adelaide Test of the Bodyline series. Someone had let the world know that Plum Warner had gone to commiserate with Bill Woodfull over what was going on, amid the bruises and the disaffection, out there. Woodfull's reply has long since gone into the treasure chest of sport's most acrid memories. 'There are two teams out there - one is playing cricket and the other is not.' At the time it was intended as no more than one man's despairing and confidential thoughts to another. Instead, it made international headlines.

Official response was one of considerable anger. There was talk of a betrayal of confidences. And fingers pointed savagely at Fingleton. As the only professional journalist in the Australian team, he was the obvious suspect. He was questioned, and denied being the informant. Indeed he maintained his innocence until the day he died; he was actually to imply in print that Bradman was more culpable.

That one incident in a sweaty and resentful dressing-room at Adelaide was without doubt the source of so much of the simmering misery, on personal levels, that kept resurfacing. 'This was a bloody injustice - I was blamed for something I didn't do.'

Over the years the Australian dressing-room was oddly bisected. It was partly a religious divide, with Fingo and his fellow Catholics in one camp. I heard too a theory, which I'm not sure can be substantiated, that there was also a Masonic exclusivity among the 'coffins' and the discarded bats and pads.

Fingleton could be small-minded and less than generous to Bradman in some of the published work. He would also, when in a more congenial writing mood, go out of his way to praise the feats of brilliance of 'this great technician . . . the man who at lunch is working out what his score will be at tea . . .', and the Don's varying examples of graciousness.

The trouble was that Fingo was convinced Bradman didn't like him. The mutual wariness never disappeared. Fingleton didn't waste an opportunity in print to dwell on Bradman's less endearing traits - the apparent meanness in not buying a round when he'd just been given a £1,000 cheque, the remoteness, the ruthless streak.

Fingleton did not approve of the way the West Indian bowlers deliberately pitched short. He was just as scathing about the bouncers from Lindwall and Miller, aimed at Hutton and Compton, in 1948. He held Bradman responsible for the resurgent animosity, and quoted him instructing Miller to 'grind the English Test players into the dust'. Bradman would take exception, maybe with good cause, at some of the things that Fingo wrote.

I have in front of me a letter written by Fingleton to a good friend at Downside, the Roman Catholic school in Somerset. It refers to the special dinner held to commemorate the Centenary Test at Melbourne in 1977.

Bradman spoke for too long. He tried to cover the whole hundred years, speaking for about 45 minutes. Bill O'Reilly's comment was that it was 40 minutes too long . . . there was also what some saw as a cheap sneer at Denis Compton's various marriages, a reference which Denis very much resented as he was entitled to do . . . I noticed that chaps like Larwood, Voce, Ian Chappell, Stackpole, Compton and others did not stand up in the ovation to the great man for his speech. I stood for the speech, not the man.

Friends would try continuously to persuade Fingleton to shut past differences, seeming at times to be verging on paranoia, from his mind.

One of those friends was John Woodcock, with whom he stayed

at lovely Longparish, during his last tour of this country. The ageing, still twinkling Australian was especially relaxed in the Hampshire village. He talked cricket endlessly, spicing the evenings with priceless anecdotes, in the warm companionship of *The Times'* erstwhile cricket 'maestro' (as Fingo used to call him). He liked Longparish: the villagers, the pub only a last-orders stroll from John's home, reading the names on the old gravestones, gazing over the gate at the local cricket pitch.

'I was very fond indeed of him. When he last stayed, he showed me the relevant chapter on Sir Don for the forthcoming book. I shook my head and did my best to dissuade him, saying nothing would be achieved. He may have watered his comments down a bit from the proof stage - but he just wouldn't let go. It was such a pity.'

We have contemplated him as the private, brooding man. Yet in an intriguingly paradoxical spirit, he rather liked - whatever the superficial protestations - celebrity status. This came late to him, with his appearance on the Michael Parkinson TV shows in Australia and here. He was quite a performer, a natural in front of the cameras. He was clever enough to polish a penetrative phrase in advance. He knew how to project his dry wit. Cricket and politics that backed away from the establishment stance gave him an easy rapport with Parkinson. Strong opinions and sly, Aussie quips were everything that a chat show demanded.

His appearances on the box in this belated role made him more of a celebrity at home, where his standing, as a commentator on cricketing matters for instance, was less evident than in this country.

This public side of him, when he could quite mesmerically hold the stage, made him a popular dinner guest. He liked a good port and the stories rattled away through the covers and into the early hours. His rather gruff, no-fawning delivery oscillated from the trenchant to, more often, the hilarious. He was goaded to dispense

—

the gossip - and he seldom failed to respond.

In England, he was happiest of all in the West Country. Somerset was his favourite county. He used to say all the Australian tourists wanted to play at Taunton: it ensured that they'd be in batting form in time for the next Test. He liked to tease his hosts with digs at native sporting virtues.

It isn't quite true that Dickens brought Fingo and John Luff together. One of the Australian's earliest possessions, in terms of literature, was an old copy of *Pickwick Papers*. Luff, known by Fingleton as 'the Squire of Litton' (a small village near Chewton Mendip, in Somerset) helps to run his own Pickwick Club and indeed adopts the figuratively bewhiskered persona of Mr Pickwick. He's also devoted to Somerset cricket and became the county president in 1991. He claims to have admired Fingleton ever since he saw him taken in the slips by Hammond off Wellard in the 1938 Test.

Compared with the political philosophy of Luff, Fingleton was positively mellow and thoroughly radical.

'Trouble with you, Luff, is that you're High Tory. Should have come out with Cook. Wouldn't be surprised if you keep slaves.'

It was said with a delayed smile. Some people found him too acerbic, Luff realised long ago that the humour predominated; the Australian could laugh at himself.

'We were eating at Bruno's in Bath. My stepdaughter, Jane, was with a French girl who knew nothing of cricket. She turned to Jane and asked: "Who's that Australian?"

'"It's Jack Fingleton. He's really quite famous. He once scored four Test centuries in a row. Spent nearly two days at the wicket."

'"Hasn't he got anything better to do?"' asked the ingenuous Gallic guest, out of Jack's hearing. When he was told, he roared with laughter.

Mrs Jessie Bradman must have felt rather the same on the

afternoon she was in the box at Lord's. A boorish brigadier was sitting next to the ubiquitous Luff, ranting on about Bradman - his attitude to the game and the way he played it.

'I feel damned sorry for anyone married to him.'

Jessie Bradman heard it, exchanged a gentle smile with one or two others, and said nothing.

Luff's relationship with Fingo - his late wife, Edith, was another devoted friend and actually attended the memorial service in Australia - was perhaps in danger of being strained a little during the last occasion the cricket writer stayed at Litton. There had been several rather boisterous house parties.

The weary Fingleton was to complain to a clerical friend: 'He does not seem to get it into his head that I'm an invalid these days. On several nights, he and others came up to my bedroom and made one heck of a noise, saying: "Let's get old Fingo out of bed." That might have passed in one of your lower-form rags but I saw little sense in it . . . There had, of course, been drink.'

One of Fingo's constant friends in England was Father Martin Salmon, then a housemaster at Downside and before that a naval officer, who has already appeared in these pages - in different context and cast list. He and Fingleton used to talk cricket and theology with equal fervour. They also played golf together.

At the Burnham-on-Sea course, in Somerset, they got as far as the sixteenth hole, dominated by a central bunker. Fingo landed just short. He surveyed the hazardous state of the grass short of the bunker. At the same time, his thoughts were on the controversial Headingley pitch he'd just left behind. Bert Lock had been called in; something called *fuserium fungus* had been diagnosed. The Test finished with two days spare.

'Dom, you must have had that groundsman from Leeds down here,' Fingo said, with a final, withering look at Burnham's savaged grass.

There was one major reservation in Father Martin's regard for his companion's journalistic prowess. He knew that Fingo had a penchant for cricket's strange little cameos. So where was the paragraph of eccentric record to denote the Downside monk's singularly rare dismissal - 'caught and bowled off head'? He went for the pull, top-edged onto his head, and the bowler, though others were lined up for the dolly, took the return catch. Fingo was watching the Ravens that day but nothing appeared in print.

'I was a bit miffed about that,' said the clerical batsman.

Fingleton would go to mass at Downside or the local parish church. He saw his visits to Somerset as therapeutic, 'somewhere to unbutton'. His singing in church was 'well above average'. It had always been rated, of course, in the pre-war Aussie team sing-songs.

His religion was strong. He was particularly philosophical in one impassioned, rambling piece he wrote for the newspapers:

I claim that cricket is the most Christian and linking sport devised by mortal man . . . There is in the charm of cricket something difficult to define, yet known to those who play and live it . . . In its culture and charm, it is based on Christian ethics. At the game's end, a man can consult his conscience. Did I give the game my best? Did I try to bluff the umpire? Did I selfishly hog the strike? Was I charitable to the successes of others? Did I keep the little woman a waiting martyr in the post-match jollities? All these and others, and with my career ended, I strike my breast and say: *Mea culpa, mea maxima culpa.*

We know what is right. If we don't do it, we don't delude ourselves. We know.

A revealing miscellany of spontaneous self-examination: and at least one stray pang of guilt.

Fingleton's upbringing had been both faithful and frugal. There

—

were invariably enough priests around, back in Sydney or when he went around the world, to keep him thinking. But he had the facility to harness an adept pragmatism to the basic precepts of his faith. In the mid-Sixties he had taken Belinda with him to St Peter's, in Rome, for a mass celebrated by Pope Paul V1. The trouble was they had no tickets. So they took up positions optimistically in the nave.

It was no time to be too coy and backward, even in a famous place of worship. He sized up the possibilities, worked out who was seeing the dignitaries to the best seats, and caught his eye. Before too long both Belinda and her father were in what he described later as ringside seats. He had discreetly handed over a few lira to the susceptible attendant, but argued that a little corruption was justified, even at St Peter's.

Just as the deprivations of home life in the early days helped to bolster his religion, so they shaped his political beliefs. Sir Robert Menzies used to say he was Labour but in truth he never officially belonged to any party. He was friendly with politicians of high office; they belonged to both main parties.

His father had graduated from tram driver to MP. He'd been a good trade unionist, having no truck either with avaricious bosses or the demon drink. The son, who had left school at fourteen and was largely self-educated in the way of so many boys and girls of the time, did the rounds in various newspaper offices. The sweep from copy-book to political commentator and confidant of prime minsters gave him scoops. Certainly one or two were impressed by his cricketing pedigree. In the style of the contentious lobby system, he was never short of non-attributable quotes or often newsworthy ones 'on the record'. A number of his colleagues, on rival papers, were envious of his success rate.

He was imbued with a sturdy, old-fashioned sense of ethics in journalism - as in sport. He despised bowlers intent on causing

—

pain. He despised those who intimidated or cheated. Just as vehemently, he hated veiled suggestions that he might compromise something he was proposing to write. There was the time Menzies, who should have known better, was ingenuous enough to ask Fingo to shop a few of his fellow reporters. 'Stuff that for a bloody lark,' he told the Prime Minister.

In England he was fascinated by the House of Commons and the machinations in the Chamber. Those were the days when rival politicians were more willing to share a drink, only minutes after clashing vitriolically over a sensitive party issue.

The Rt Hon Denis Howell, Labour's former Sports Minister, first met Fingleton at a Test match. He invited him to the House for a meal. Howell, himself a former Football League referee, is also a vice-president of Warwickshire CCC. 'I introduced him to the Prime Minister, Harold Wilson. It wasn't so much a formal introduction - they sort of bumped into each other and I think it was a particular delight for Jack.' The Prime Minister was also genuinely interested in cricket.

Fingo used his press pass to sit in the gallery of the House several times. He was absolutely absorbed by the debates - and Commons ritual. 'I was struck by his inquiring mind. He wanted to know so much about how we did things. As for his political stance, I should say definitely left of centre in terms of Australian politics,' said Howell.

A few days before Fingleton died, Denis Howell was in Australia, heading a parliamentary delegation. After some difficulty, he managed to get hold of Jack's telephone number and rang him. They talked, Fingleton weakly, for fifteen minutes or so. His parting words were: 'Give my regards to Michael Parkinson'. He'd really loved those chat shows.

What I remember vividly about Jack Fingleton, quite apart from the wisdom he imparted and the personalised way he contributed to the general bonhomie of the cricket press box, was his cussed streak. He would suddenly make a challenging remark, quite gratuitously, and if it didn't meet with any marked response, he'd go into a long silence.

He probably sulked. Didn't he once irritate the crowd at Trent Bridge, in 1938, by sitting down at the wicket when he was being given the slow handclap for some prolonged obduracy?

And what do we make of what happened at Sydney a few years earlier, when he badly needed runs to clinch a tour place (which didn't materialise in any case)? He was nervous and suffering from cramp, which possibly excused some careless sparring and a simple chance to slips not accepted. In his embarrassment, he wandered down the wicket to prod an imaginary divot. The wicket-keeper, Ben Barnett, had no qualms: he flicked off the bails.

Bemused and cross with himself - no doubt, initially, with Barnett too - Fingleton set off with glum expression toward the pavilion. Woodfull called him back, saying the decision would be reversed. There was some huffing and puffing before Fingo relented and continued his innings.

He was later criticised for not accepting Woodfull's generosity straightaway. But he was faced, after all, with a tricky technicality and his prickly temperament was telling him: 'If Barnett wants to get me out that way, then I'll bloody well go.'

In fact, he later went to pains to exonerate the wicket-keeper who, he said, was absolutely entitled to take the bails off.

As a writer, Fingleton's style varied from the rigidly formal, on occasions, to the racy. The prose was opinionated because that was the man. He loathed the growing intrusion of commercialism in sport and said so with dismissive contempt. He often confided that he wished he could write as well as Cardus. At times he did; he certainly had more respect for the literal truth.

He had an intimate knowledge of the mechanics of his chosen

—

craft - unlike some of those irritating essayists, who fashioned their leisured, weekly pieces with obscure classical allusions and affected metaphors, and deigned to sit with busy, deadline-conscious hacks. He wasn't averse to a bit of good, old human interest in his cabled narrative. When Benaud, the Aussie captain of 1961 - and a practitioner of the same journalistic trade - was coming up with as many angles as wickets for the appreciative press corps, Fingleton would chuckle and help himself. At the same time, he didn't much like the direction sporting journalism was going. He hated the increasing insistence by sports editors on 'nannies' (quotes: rhyming slang).

He was just as scornful about book editors who chose to chop 20,000 words off his Trumper publication, or desk-bound newspapermen who revised his copy. It didn't often happen. He used to say: 'If Jim Swanton has an arrangement that his words aren't altered at all, so should I'. It wasn't so much arrogance, more a belief that if he'd taken the trouble to make a point in a particular way, it should be left alone.

His relationship with *The Sunday Times* was a mutually productive one. The paper was proud of its respected, literate and entertaining contributor. He was never a boring writer. If he could come up with a political exclusive, so much the better. On his visits to England, he was a favoured guest at the *Sunday Times* lunches. He got on well with Harold Evans. The fact that one was the son of a tram driver and the other of a train driver probably gave them a common bond. Fingo enjoyed the flattery at the lunches. In his greenhorn days, he'd have been happiest of all working for the *Manchester Guardian*, maybe even to sit in the same office as Cardus. He now had real professional clout of his own, especially in his part-time, well-displayed employment for *The Sunday Times*, and it impressed those at home.

Many were surprised when the liaison came to an end. Suddenly he was appearing in the columns of *The Observer* instead. The reasons for his move never fully became public knowledge, but he was known to dislike the way *The Sunday Times* was, more and more, treating sport. A colleague told me: 'Jack thought they were getting altogether too analytical . . . too many diagrams, too much theory and academic discussion . . . He didn't think sport was a matter to be taken quite as intensely.'

Some thought they detected, real or imagined, a hint of rivalry with Robin Marlar, the paper's No 1 cricket writer. Could Fingo even have been a little jealous of him? He wrote:

They have given me great space lately but I notice that whenever I spread my wings, Robin does also in a nearby column. It seems he has an arrangement with them that he must be up with me. That is fair enough because of his position. But I found it difficult to do the last tour with him. He seems on edge and not to like Australians - and he flies off his rocker too easily for my liking. He is over-sensitive to any criticism of himself and I had mixed thoughts when I read him on Mike Denness recently. He gave the Scot more stick than most.

There was something of the Fingleton make-up in the manner he offered his services to the *Sunday Times*' traditional rival. The sports editor at that time, the affable Peter Corrigan, received the first unsolicited article from him and assumed it had been sent to the wrong paper. Then he read the accompanying letter - and couldn't wait to publish.

We have touched on his mischievous skills as a raconteur and gossip. 'Hey, Fingo, tell us what really happed to Bill Edrich on the plane that time.'

'Ah, yes, I won't forget that Qantas trip. Dear old Bill, in his haste to make fun with the good cheer, over-imbibed and fell all over the incumbent Arlott who dotted him one. Great start. No other blows that I heard of, though I'm not up to date on the trip back, John is now known to me as the Aylesford Mauler . . .'

This is not intended in any sense as a comprehensive portrait of a gifted, no doubt underrated, Test cricketer who played for New South Wales between 1929-40. There are plenty of books, some written with laudable modesty by himself ('I wasn't a terribly good batsman but I fancied myself as a fielder') that tell us how he fared as a player.

There were eighteen Tests, his four consecutive hundreds for his country, his famous 346-run stand with Bradman, when we cannot be sure how much they said to each other as they kept crossing in mid-wicket. He made runs at his own pace, without being able to play the pull. As a fielder, he stood unflinchingly at short leg for his great pal Bill O'Reilly. He patrolled the covers and the outfield with equal vigilance.

He sang less after the stroke he suffered, and the vigour of his writing understandably tailed off. In the box, he was a mellower companion. His kindly guidance to younger occupants, like Scyld Berry, then with him at *The Observer*, was valued. He died in a Sydney hospital following a heart attack, aged seventy-three.

Perhaps they always appreciated him more in this country, especially in the West where he got to know the farmers, the Chewton Mendip butchers like Pete Denning's father, Tom, and the chefs at the Castle in Taunton, where whortleberry pie was always specifically on the menu for the Australian cricketers.

'I'm back hure again,' he'd say, affecting an accent of Blackdown or Quantocks pedigree.

One thing is for sure. If he had been around as a player over the last decade or so, some of his more affluent mates around the Mendips would have persuaded him to play for Somerset. It wouldn't have been too difficult.

—

FOUR

BILL ANDREWS

Twelve O'Clock Low

Andrews, William Harry Russell.
Born Swindon, Wiltshire, 1908.
Died Weston-super-Mare,
Somerset, 1990.
Somerset (1930-47, 226 matches).
Fast-medium bowler and hard-
hitting batsman who achieved the
double twice before the war.
Became county coach and
passionate committee man.

BILL ANDREWS WAS SACKED four times by Somerset, twice as a player and twice as a coach. It may have been more. Everything about Bill was bounteous: especially his heart. But snubs were forgotten as quickly as yesterday's match. His all-consuming affection for the county never wavered.

Well into his seventies, he phoned me early one morning and whispered down the phone from his home in Weston-super-Mare: 'For heaven's sake, don't tell Ennyd - I'm thinking of applying once more for the job of coach. And I'll manage 'em, too, if they'll let me.' It wasn't the moment to tell him to forget it. His head was buzzing with erstwhile excitement at the thought of a working return to Taunton, however absurdly unrealistic the notion was.

Maybe his tolerant, long-suffering wife had still eavesdropped and dissuaded him. The application was never posted to the county authorities which had done their best, over the years, to become impervious to his whims, excesses and instinctive enthusiasms.

Somerset cricket was the mistress he could never get out his system. He quarrelled with her when he thought she was making a fool of herself. There were tiffs and reconciliations. In her presence, he could be dotty with adulation.

He was a big, gangling, handsome man who would monopolise a crowded bar with his booming conviviality. In that natural habitat, his engaging masculinity was manifested in the way he puffed his battered briar and in the positive, often hilarious, views he held with such overt passion, about every conceivably organic strand of the county game, from the time he worked the scoreboard as a twelve-year-old at Clarence Park. There was an apparent surfeit of self-confidence. Yet his mistress also clouded and distorted his judgment. He was blind to some of her imperfections. The abundance of his praises sprang from a

—

generosity of spirit. He coached hundreds of schoolboys, many in obscure rural playing fields as well as at Millfield. To him the best were always embryonic Huttons and Stathams.

At the time he gave up at Millfield because of ill health, the headmaster, Colin Atkinson made a speech, saying that no one had done more for the game in the West Country. 'Bill is accepted and welcomed on every county ground and is one of cricket's great personalities.'

We knew Colin said this because his words were reported in all the local papers - filed by Bill. As a self-publicist he surely had no peer. Yet he did it in a way that was utterly endearing and acceptable. He was never called boorish or boastful. The fact was that he needed recognition desperately; he needed to be in the papers, needed to be shouted at warmly across the street, needed to be joked about and admired at the same time. While still a player, he seemed to know all the influential cricket writers from Fleet Street. The result was that when Somerset were singularly mean-spirited about the terms of his testimonial, Crawford White and Alex Bannister were very soon aware of them, and were taking a popular, partial view of his plight.

Successive chairmen, secretaries and busy-body committee members came to acknowledge with grudging resignation or poor grace that they were on a loser. John Daniell was so exasperated on one occasion, according to Bill, that he bit right through his pipe. He had already run out of apposite words.

Bill, for reasons we shall discuss later, was to become paradoxically a sad figure and recluse. He spent his final years seated in an armchair at home, half-watching the horse-racing on television and choosing to have few visitors. His spirits were low, his once massive body was shrunken, and he was ready to die. He used to tell me: 'I'm going far too late - the public will have forgotten me'.

—

In fact, he died a celebrity. It is said the streets of Taunton were blocked on the day in 1931 that Sammy Woods, Somerset's boisterous and legendary digger, was buried. But he was loved no more than '12 o'clock Andrews'. ('Just look at my bowling action in all those pictures - modelled on Ted McDonald, you know.')

Bill's cremation at Weston in January 1989 was an occasion, cheerful rather than irreverent. The bulging congregation was full of old cricketers and cronies. Outside were the television crews, waiting to catch Horace Hazell and some of the others for a last embellished story. Up in the pulpit, the clergyman kept the anecdotes going. None of it was misplaced. The local papers had led their back pages with news of his death. 'END OF SOMERSET LEGEND'. Andrews, briefly a fully paid up member of the NUJ, couldn't have done it better himself.

Maybe I should declare an interest in the old rascal. From the day I saw my first Somerset match in the late Thirties he was destined to be one of my imperishable heroes. I can still see him walking off the field, at the aircraft factory ground in Yeovil, a dangling, bronzed arm round the neck of the man he in turn idolised, Arthur Wellard. Two giants, with their nut-brown faces and sweat coursing its way down their crafty, imposing features. To me they were always in tandem, inseparable in my imagination. They might have been twins; it meant nothing to me that they swung the ball in opposite directions or that Bill at least had his own teeth. Wellard would mischievously take his out on a hot afternoon, as he fielded at silly mid-off, to the consternation of batsmen not endowed with a similar sense of humour.

Bill was the unsophisticated junior clerk, in a solicitor's office, who started his career as a cricket pro, cutting the grass and coaching the local lads from the twine works at my native village of East Coker a year after I was born. He it was I invited back, as principal guest, at my village club's annual dinner soon after the war. It was a spectacular return. He dallied in Yeovil - on market day when the pubs stayed open - and then absent-mindedly set light to the artificial fireplace in the hotel where the dinner was being held. In the years that followed, he was to become friend and confidant.

He asked me to edit his book, *The Hand That Bowled Bradman*, published in 1973. The second hardest part was to reduce his exuberant, rambling narrative of 160,000 words down to 60,000. The hardest was to persuade him, at the very last moment, to go through with the project. Suddenly he was on the phone. 'We've got to stop it - I just can't go through with it . . . I'm in a dreadful state . . . I'm confused . . . Can't remember if half the stories are true . . . I'm afraid of offending people . . .' And so on.

I'd seen and talked to him at some of his low points. This was the worst. I motored straight over to his home, where I found him acutely depressed and withdrawn. He'd been worrying about the book all night, could see legal repercussions that I knew didn't exist. He was adamant. Would I ring Macdonald's for him and stop the printing which was due the following week.

Now I can't be sure that every anecdote about his beloved contemporaries carried the literal truth. But they were neither malicious nor defamatory, I assured him. After some agonising introspection and recurrent pipe-filling, he finally accepted it was too late to stop the imminent print-run at Purnell's in those pre-Maxwell days. I fancy that with a little technical wizardry, we managed to change a couple of stories and even to pull one out altogether.

The Hand That Bowled Bradman, memories of a professional cricketer, with a foreword by John Arlott - one of so many who stayed with Bill and consumed excessive quantities of Ennyd's exceptional homemade wine - was published to much critical acclaim. The Cricket Society nominated it as second only to Jim Swanton's book in that particular year.

I had known for some time that Bill was a manic depressive, a secret successfully kept from the majority of his doting fans. The mental illness, apt to surface in the spring just as it did with the tragic Harold Gimblett, was almost impossible to equate with the bubbling, stammering centre-stage persona, whose name was rarely absent from the West Country sports pages, and whose quaint, diffuse oratorical style, laden with indiscretion and apocryphal diversions, entranced hundreds of cricket dinners. (His favourite opening was: 'Hope I have a bit more luck than last night. Had to speak in Wells. Had the B-Bishop of Bath and Wells on one side of me and the Abbot of Downside on the other. P-P-Put my new wristwatch down on the table when I started. It had gone by the time I finished . . .')

That was the happy, familiar side of Andrews. But he wrote me dozens of copious letters over the years and they dwelt increasingly with his depression, less with his cricket.

I have a letter he wrote back in the early Seventies when the idea for the book was taking shape. The handwriting is beautiful: no question of a ball-point pen. Couched in conspiratorial tone, it begins:

The wife has gone out so it gives me a chance to confide. I am feeling a lot worse and have now got to the point where I sneak out of the house with the dog, along the golf links, hiding from everyone. That will tell you the state I'm in . . . My mind has gone a blank. I am not sleeping now - only about two or three hours a night - and I'm taking my tablets as fast as I can. Oh David, I'm terrible. Ennyd has been wonderful, putting up with me as usual. She'll pull me through . . .

—

She had been a nurse, engaged to a doctor. Her first meeting with Bill was in London at a cricket match where ironically both men were playing. She gradually became aware, after her marriage to Bill, of his 'highs and lows'. And because of her experience in nursing, she was better able to cope than some wives would have been. At his lowest, he would cry for days. Ennyd would say quietly: 'If you want to cry, cry. That will do no harm. Get it out of your system.'

It mystified her why he was at his worst in the springtime, 'when life was surging'. The black spells would last for two months or more. Yet, in a strange way, he was at times easier to live with when depressed. She found him quite exhausting when he was on a high. 'I just waited for him to come down, even though it made me feel guilty.'

For all his extrovert mannerisms - and the general regional acclaim which he devoured - he did suffer, Ennyd perceptively suggests, from a genuine inferiority complex. He often felt, however impressive his county record as an all-rounder, that he should have done better as a player - and made more money as a part-time businessman. He used to claim, without too much evidence, that Wally Hammond vetoed his one chance for a Test place. In his early days he carried a social chip and did not warm to some of those amateurs who, because of their better education and enunciation, kept him and fellow pros out of the side in the vacation period.

There was mental instability in the family. His father, once a pub landlord in Swindon, spent some time in a mental hospital. Bill's wife suggested the father should be brought out to spend his final weeks in Weston. There was plenty of time to ponder, and he did, on his father's condition. 'But as far as I know he'd never seen a dead body and was far too frightened to go near him in the end.'

—

Then came, in the autumn of 1977, the death of his son from his first marriage. Michael was a popular police constable. He was found lying on rocks below the Esplanade near the Anchor Hotel, Weston. There were severe head injuries and he was dead by the time the ambulance got him to hospital.

Michael had been transferred from Taunton to Weston only a short time before and was living with his mother. The evidence at the inquest made it clear that his marriage was going wrong; his wife and eleven-year-old son had left home. The once easy-going Somerset policeman was described as 'very depressed'. He had a spell in a hospital, receiving treatment for this condition. The coroner recorded an open verdict. Bill was convinced it was suicide. 'This bloody depression - it runs in the family,' he told me.

Bill was also dreadfully affected, whatever the front he put on, by his drink-driving conviction. He had always been a hard drinker. Why else would he have pitched his tent alongside the beer marquee at Clacton during his playing days? His gestures became more and more expansive, his tales more surreal and his voice louder. But he was usually well in control.

He and Ennyd were coming back from a singularly generous-flowing reception, being given by the Showerings drinks company for the Australian tourists during their match at Taunton. It was a glamorous setting: buffet around an indoor pool, and a band on the lawn. Bill's wife still recalls the nightmare events that followed with chilling clarity.

'As we left the reception I looked at Bill and thought, "Oh, my God, he's drunk". It was all that champagne. I begged for us to find somewhere locally to stay or sleep in the car. On the ride back to Weston, I eventually asked him to stop. I got into the back of the car and put a coat over my head . . . We got right to the top of Milton Hill, just round the corner from our home, when Bill crashed into a lamp-post.

'He wasn't hurt. I told him to go straight home and not answer the door to anyone. I also suggested that he should say I was the driver - though I couldn't even drive a car.' Ennyd broke her elbow and was in hospital for a week. Bill was charged.

In court, one of the magistrates said at the commencement of the case: 'I think I should say I know Mr Andrews very well.'

The chairman, another Weston woman, added: 'We all know Mr Andrews very well.'

Bill felt it was time to contribute to the judicial conversation. 'I don't think it really matters, I'm pleading guilty.' The Bench imposed a lenient fine of £25 and banned him for a year. The experience was shattering for him. A sensitive and sensible man, he admitted to friends that he was thoroughly ashamed about what had happened. Drink-driving carried a particular stigma and he worried over the reaction of the local community. For once it was publicity that left him embarrassed, guilty and fearful about what his friends would think. At this stage he was beginning to withdraw from people. He was now turning down invitations to club dinners and even dissuading old acquaintances from calling.

He started brooding more. The deaths of cricketers he had played with compounded his dispirited state. Wellard had always been the one he looked up to. Bill had envied Arthur his flashy suits, his skill at cards, his penchant for National Hunt and the dogs. They drank and roomed together on away matches. Bill wryly forgave him for the cunning way he invariably ensured he had the choice of ends, leaving Bill to bowl his in-swingers into the wind. In another letter to me, Andrews recalled a match in 1932 at Kettering when he and Wellard figured in a formidable though odd batting stand. In a high-scoring game on a placid wicket, Somerset were left to play only for first innings points - after centuries by Vallance Jupp for Northants and Dickie

Burrough for the West Country side.

'When the last over was called, we needed just one to tie and two to win. But Arthur, the slogger, had for some reason gone into his shell. He'd gone into a bit of a trance, not realising that the close on the third day was six p.m., and he wasn't taking any notice of my frantic gestures. Matthews bowled that final over - and Arthur, to my horror, let the first three balls pass outside the off stump. The next three were played defensively. I ask you.'

The Somerset skipper, Reggie Ingle, was pretty livid. He blamed Bill for not goading his partner into action. 'I was dropped for the next match. And bang went my home match fee of £6.' Again Wellard was quickly forgiven; such was idolatry.

Arthur's death in 1981 deeply grieved Bill. 'I went with Horace Hazell and Tom Tout, our scorer, to the funeral. Only a dozen males were present, no women. It was a little church in the middle of a huge cemetery. As far as I could see, the only official representative of cricket present was someone from Kent. No one from MCC or other counties. I've just had two large glasses of elderberry wine so please excuse the writing.'

As far as I could see it was as neat and flowing as ever. But Bill needed those drinks. He had seen the scant recognition at Wellard's funeral as a slight. Did great old cricketers really die forgotten, he was asking himself?

The death of Spud, his faithful Irish cross-bred dog, was another fearful and untimely blow. Apart from the family which he loved, Bill looked upon Spud as his most constant and loyal friend. They walked miles together, when Bill was going through his blackest days. The old cricketer would slump on the bank and mumble his despair to his little companion. Worlebury, where the Andrews lived, was covered with snow when the dog died. A taxi was needed to get through the drifts and take Spud to the vet to be put down.

For years they had seemed to be inseparable: as Bill walked the mile or so to the bay to put down his nets in search of sole, mullet and dabs, or hake in the winter; as he went off in September to pick elderberries, blackberries and rose hips for Ennyd's wine; as he stumbled unseeingly round the golf links and local lanes in pursuit of an elusive mental peace.

A neighbour told me of an occasion when Bill was so low that he simply could not bring himself to go home. Instead he slept, for a few troubled hours, on the neighbour's front-room sofa. There were philosophical asides and soliloquies to his younger friend during that tormented night. The next morning, he whispered his thanks and crept out, Spud reassuringly at his heels.

In addition to his depression, his general health deteriorated. He had serious problems with the veins on his leg ('My bloody legs have gone on me at last, David - all that pounding up the wicket I did for Jack White and the others') and resulting ulcers. He spent a Christmas in hospital when he wanted to be with his family. He talked of a duodenal ulcer that was always threatening to resurface after he'd had a little too much to drink. There was increasing concern by him about his health. Some of his fears, his wife believed, were psychosomatic. I come back to another letter he wrote: 'I have not got long to go. I suspect the doctor and the specialist have given me up - and the doctor is a personal friend.'

So was his dentist. And surely, in any study of this big-hearted, ebullient - at least to the public - sportsman, it is time to return to the quintessential humour that hummed and sparked wherever he stepped with that loping stride and in those outsized shoes.

Simon Wotton lived near Bill. He was a fine hockey player, at county and divisional level. He went to grammar school with Brian Rose and Bill's son, Mark, and was very much a friend of

—

the family. His father was also Bill's dentist for well over twenty years. Simon remembers an occasion when Andrews arrived unannounced at the foot of the stairs to the surgery, oblivious to the fact that there was already a patient in the chair.

'Hey, Bruce, you up there? It's the bloody bottom one which is hurting.' Then, ignoring token protests from the receptionist, he marched upstairs into the surgery.

'Look, Bruce,' he said, withdrawing the blackened old pipe and opening his mouth, 'it's that bugger down there.'

Simon was one of many, certainly not just in hilly, bracing Worlebury towering over the Bristol Channel, who revered Andrews. He got Bill's autograph - none of the thousands asked in vain - when he was twelve. He worked the scoreboard at Clarence Park, just as his hero had done years before.

It was Simon and his wife whom Bill persuaded to drive him to Sophia Gardens, Cardiff, for a John Player match. His planned lift had not materialised and he was quite agitated. That big, ungainly frame clambered into the car. Relieved and immediately relaxed, he lit his pipe and in no time the car windows were steamed up.

A long queue at the Severn Bridge delayed the journey and Bill was soon making it clear that he had taken a pint or two that lunchtime and now badly needed to go to the toilet. They somehow got to the entrance of the ground, but the passenger could wait no longer. He bundled out and, in the Gallic fashion, went behind the nearest tree trunk. The good-natured Welsh spectators, piling into the Gardens, discreetly ignored him.

Then the car was parked and Bill announced to Simon and his wife: 'Leave it to me - I'll get you in.' Hadn't Colin Atkinson said, in that valedictory speech of his, that Bill was welcomed on every ground in the country?

The blustering Andrews' charm worked. The gateman

accepted it was family. And the irresistible blarney continued as Bill moved up to the balcony, introducing Wilf Wooller to 'my daughter and son-in-law'. That was something of a miscalculation. Wilf had already met Bill's daughter, Sara. Never too averse to a shaft of resourcefulness, the Guru of Glamorgan winked and remained untypically quiet.

There are countless stories of the Somerset man's cheeky enterprise, all told with equal affection. It was said that he never once entered a West Country pub, however remote the hamlet, without being instantly recognised and having a foaming pint of strong ale hurriedly put on the counter for him. The big palm was ritualistically extended in all directions. 'Shake the hand that bowled Bradman,' he'd sing out in throaty corporate greeting. There was rarely need for him to put his hand into his own pocket all night.

On the return journey to Somerset once, with his Under-19 side, he stopped his car as soon as he reached the county boundary and decided on the spot how he could avoid a long additional drive to Glastonbury with one of the team. He flagged down the first vehicle going in that direction. 'I want you to give a ride to this young man,' he told the startled motorist. 'He's one of Somerset's finest cricketers of the future. You'll feel very privileged to have him in the car.' It worked as usual. To Andrews, mention of Somerset cricket was the spiritual passport that could not fail. His own personality was almost hypnotic. One could see how the later years became so poignantly bereft.

He was perhaps the most popular figure Somerset cricket ever had. Certainly Sammy Woods, who also liked the raucous chatter of a skittle alley and possessed the classless bonhomie that becomes an Aussie, was his only rival. Lionel Palairet's popularity was largely confined to the hotel lounge and hunting lodge, Gimblett's to the Taunton (and Frome) grounds and fourth-form

—

romance, Farmer White's to the harvest suppers around the Quantocks, and Botham's to the pulp forests of the tabloid devotees.

Yet Andrews remained unfulfilled. The chairmanship of the county's cricket committee eluded him, despite his incessant lobbying and all the self-projection in the local papers. And, on an infinitely more personal level, his impassioned hope that his son, Mark, would follow him into county cricket was never going to be attained.

The filial aspirations were unyielding. Mark was a moderate player. He dutifully went to the Somerset nets at Christmas time. He played 2nd XI for Millfield and Weston. 'Dad was always watching and hoping, even at primary school in Uphill where he came to do some coaching. There was a Somerset Under-15 trial at Weston and although I was too young, Dad arranged for me to take part. I also played for Somerset Under-19, but only because Dad was in charge and picked the team.

'All he wanted was for me to be a success at cricket. He wouldn't have minded if I'd spent the winters digging the road for the council in Weston provided I played for Somerset in the summer. He pushed cricket down my throat - and I never enjoyed it until the pressure was off and I realised I was not going to be much good at it. Until then he was always throwing the ball to me. Expecting far too much of me.'

Mark was a better rugby player. He played in the pack at Millfield, in the same team as J.P.R. Williams. Earlier, while still going to school in Weston, Mark was doing a paper round for pocket money. 'Dad offered to pay me the money not to do the round - he didn't want me to get up early in the morning.' After a late night, with Mark still in bed when his friends called for him, Bill would say: 'You can't wake him'. He was incredibly protective.

—

So he was in the case of Sara. He encouraged her to score in turn for the youth side, Somerset Under-19 and then the county 2nd X1. 'Dad used to say it was part of my education, being chatted up by twenty-two young players. But at the same time, Brian Rose would say that Dad used to sit on the hotel stairs outside my room, for away games, to make absolutely sure nothing happened to me.'

Bill was put in charge on one occasion when Ennyd and Mark were on holiday. Sara, an attractive sixteen-year-old at Weston School for Girls, went to a party given by some boys from the Technical School. 'Don't worry, Dad, it's all so innocent. No drink and I'll be staying with my best friend overnight.'

It wasn't quite that innocent and Sara panicked when she heard her father's voice at the front door. He dragged Sara, as well as her friend, away. Later that night, he gave Sara a box of chocolates. 'Sorry, Sar, I just can't take that kind of responsibility when your mother isn't here.'

His speeches at cricket dinners all round the country were legendary - either outrageously funny and spontaneous, or unmitigated disasters. He made few notes, relying on his treasury of stories about his contemporaries or those who came after. He had a tale about almost every one of them. Most were acceptably slanderous. Ennyd remembers when once he'd gone to pains at a rather formal dinner to type out a quite lengthy speech. Suddenly, a third of the way through, he threw his sheets of paper on the table. 'You don't want to hear all this. I've given it to the papers - and you can read it in the morning, if you've got nothing better to do.'

His indiscretions were plentiful. Judgment was never one of his reliable qualities. No one ever knew what he was going to say next, especially if the host club had been generous with the drinks. As the guest of honour at one established club in the area, he told his audience: 'One of your teams came second in the league - and I'm sure you'd have won it if for the last six months the vice-captain hadn't been sleeping with the captain's wife.' As far as I know, no writs were flying afterwards.

On another night, he could lose his thread and ramble badly. Tony Ellis, a solicitor who once as a boy at Weston prep school was a pupil along with John Cleese of Bill's lunchtime coaching session, asked his former cricket tutor to East Anglia in the mid-Seventies to talk at two village dinners on successive nights. 'The first dinner was a great success. He had a wonderful time, making them laugh with his distinctive style of speech-making, then dancing with the wives and girlfriends. The following night he was a bit hungover. He struggled with his speech. He was well aware that he hadn't gone down terribly well, and that upset him.'

I used to get a running commentary on his speeches. 'Told 'em how much I admired Jack White but couldn't bring myself to go to his funeral' . . . 'They loved all the inside stories I rattled off about Jack Meyer, especially when I caught him out on the square getting some bowling practice at Wells long before the start - and I realised the old so-and-so was to be handed the new ball ahead of me' . . . 'They wanted to know my favourite Somerset captain and I surprised 'em by saying R-Reggie Ingle'. No of course he didn't stammer in his letters, but I imagine that was how it still occasionally came out.

William Harry Russell Andrews would surely have played for his country but for the war. He twice completed the double, took a hat-trick against Surrey and, with Bertie Buse, bowled out the Indians before lunch at Taunton just after the war. I got his autograph during the interval, and he told those of us who had queued so adoringly that he'd done it in a pair of borrowed boots. He was fast-medium, faultless in action and expansive in gesture.

—

He engendered affection around the boundary. As his son Mark put it: 'He was a pretty exceptional man - he had an influence on so many lives.'

No bad epitaph for a journeyman pro. But exceptional he was. He loved humanity and played his artisan heart out. This he did with some versatility. He kept goal at water polo for Weston, played No 8 for the local rugby club, centre half in Western League football and strolled across the road from his home to slice his drives with undiminished joy. He once sang in the church choir at St Paul's along with brother Jack. He stood for the Ratepayers Association and dared to stick up a Labour Party poster on his garage door to support a friend. He spread his warmth and cherished bluster in all directions. His aphorisms were much quoted. 'You're a beauty,' he said to someone, most days.

At the end he was a bag of bones, hunched in a blue high-necked jersey that made him look like a cadaverous old salt. His appetite had long gone: so had his prodigious thirst. One year his wife made 273 gallons of homemade wine. There was no room for a car in the garage.

In the final years the door bell would ring. 'Don't answer it', Bill would say. The phone would go. 'Tell them I'm not up to any visits', said this once most gregarious of men. The invitations came in from the sponsors for him to attend, 'just one more time', his beloved Weston festival. He withdrew deeper into his self-imposed cavern. On his own, his memory meandered back painfully to previous Clarence Parks, when Joe Ellis perched on top of the little wooden pavilion to announce the team changes through a megaphone, and when Ernie Robson was handed a fiver from Bev and Dar Lyon's father for carting the winning six against Middlesex over the pines. And Bill cried quietly in his solitude.

—

Brian Rose, a captain of Somerset and later its cricket chairman, emotionally part of Weston-super-Mare and a steadfast friend of the Andrews family, sprinkled Bill's ashes partly on the county ground at Taunton and partly on Clarence Park. You couldn't have fairer than that.

A N D Y   D U C A T

A Fitting Exit

———

Ducat, Andrew. Born Brixton,
Surrey, 1886. Died London 1942.
Right-hand batsman. Surrey
(1906-31, 422 matches). Tests: 1.
MCC tour to Australia 1929-30.
One treble hundred and seven
double centuries. Fine footballer
who played six times for his country
and captained Aston Villa in FA
Cup Final.

IT WAS VIRTUALLY IMPOSSIBLE, as Captain Mainwaring's uncoordinated platoon often comically demonstrated, to look well dressed in Home Guard uniform. Andy Ducat managed it. When he left home at Great Enton, near Godalming, to take the train to Waterloo on 23 July 1942, the rough cloth of the private's trousers had been freshly creased.. He had polished the brasses; the forage cap, correctly aligned and angled, nestled against the right ear.

At the age of fifty-six he was still a strong man. He had slung his cricket bag up onto the rack. Daphne, his daughter and only child, sat at his side. She was proud of him: his exceptional prowess as an international cricketer and footballer, even if memories and skills were now obscured in the anonymity of just another weary-eyed man in khaki, riding with an air of contemporary resignation in a clattering stopper-train.

They kissed and parted, Daphne off to the office where she worked and Andy to Lord's. She would never see her father alive again.

He reached the ground as a member of the Surrey Home Guard team to play their Sussex counterparts. Not exactly championship vintage. But this was wartime and it was blissfully, after all, a game of cricket - and at Headquarters.

Andy looked at the typed team-sheet on the wall and allowed himself a private chuckle. Eight privates in the Surrey side . . . and a lieutenant-colonel to keep 'em in line. He was never one to bother himself too much with the implications of social divisions. For most of his life he did what he was told, whether he was being dispatched to the outfield on a scorching afternoon at The Oval or, more recently, being made rather pointlessly to order arms incessantly on drill-night. If he had views about inequalities that came from the accident of birth, he kept them to himself. He accepted that a colonel in the Home Guard would be respected, his instruction acted on, in the same way as the old pros had learned to do with tacit approval whatever their amateur skipper asked of them.

They said, in retrospect, that he was perhaps more pensive than usual as he changed. In truth he was never loquacious. He placed a faded Surrey cap over his thinning hair. The flannels were as ever immaculate. His wife, Vera, had ironed them the night before. It might almost have been for him a match from the evocative Twenties. Such felicitous habits, involving appearance and ritual, were reluctant to disappear.

Sussex won the toss and put Surrey in. Andy Ducat had left county cricket eleven years before yet was still a glamorous name, and one to savour at Lord's even at a time when the great ground was bereft of some of its grandeur and finery. He was down at No 5. 'Don't expect too many from me today,' he had said. Genuinely modest, he always said that. Even after three hundreds in a row.

He was 17 at lunch. A gentle middle-aged club cricketer's push here and there, an intuitive four through the covers. Friends remembered later that he picked at his food. During the war, players were apt to eat whatever was going, even if they were in the middle of an innings. He strapped on his pads again and went back to the wicket. In the next few overs he added another dozen runs.

Private Eaton was bowling, nothing too exacting, though he'd already taken three wickets. Ducat played him to mid-on and the ball was returned to the bowler who was just about to start his run when he saw the batsman lurch and stumble forward. He was dead by the time they carried him back to the pavilion.

The game was in the forty-fourth over. Surrey Home Guard were 132 for four. And that was when the record in *Wisden* of this modest match was poignantly and abruptly ended. Play was abandoned and the part-time soldiers silently put on their tunics again. 'Who'd have thought it of Mac?' . . . 'Always looked after himself - so fit all his life.'

At the inquest, medical evidence made it clear that he had died from heart failure and that the trusted ticker was showing all the signs of 'definite weakness'. That came as a great shock to his family. Three months earlier he had undergone a routine medical check at Eton College where he was the popular coach. 'He came home and said he was as fit as a flea and was good for another fifty years,' his daughter said.

She and her mother were later to study the photographs, taken at Lord's on the fateful day. They agreed that Mac - the name all the family and most of the cricketers used - was looking uncharacteristically strained. He seemed suddenly to be drained of the vigour and spark that had for years made him such an outstanding sportsman and had remained part of his warm persona afterwards.

His athleticism had served him so well, whether at The Oval or Villa Park. Many remembered the way he prowled the outfield, bronzed and good-looking, dark hair sleeked back. He had natural speed and elegance, in the rhythmic action of moving for the ball, scooping it up and hurling it from a distant corner straight into the gloves of the wicket-keeper. At soccer, his stamina never faltered. He surged forward from wing half; he doubled back to rectify the aberration of a teammate. Ivor Sharpe, most perceptive of football writers, used to say: 'This Ducat is so incredibly light on his feet. It's as if he's treading on air.'

Before and after the First World War, he could out-run most of his county cricket colleagues when it came to the pre-season training sessions. That, of course, was when he was around. As in the case of many of those sportsmen who excelled at both football and cricket, there could be an uneasy conflict of interests at times. It never really got resolved. County secretaries and soccer managers were often left trading insults and pulling out their hair. The respective codes blamed each other for supposedly selfish

ANDY DUCAT

attitudes. Some managers, who themselves had played both games or at least sustained an affection for the two, took a sympathetic view. That was until their player got injured playing the other game.

Andy Ducat (pronounced 'Dewkitt' by the family, 'Duckett' on the football terraces) was unlucky with injuries. When he suffered he did it with a considerate sense of democracy and balance. He missed the whole of the 1913 season with Surrey because of a broken leg. That happened at football; so had the cartilage trouble that limited his cricket the previous summer. The authorities at Surrey were apt to give him a look of veiled blackmail and say: 'We think you should give up this football nonsense, Ducat. Stick to cricket. Otherwise you'll end up a cripple.'

There were real fears about that broken leg. A silver plate was inserted in the shin bone. Recovery was slow and for a long time he hobbled around on crutches. Patience was never a problem for him. He knew that his fundamental fitness would triumph. He persevered with self-imposed exercises to build up the leg muscles again; he stripped and walked miles in the sun. Sport was his living; he never entertained the slightest notion that his double-career might be ending. By 1914 he was at Hobbs' shoulder once more. Mac's four hundreds were all modest gems, full of fluent driving, eager pulls, as well as the square and late cuts he fashioned so prettily.

His absence from the 1924 season was the result of an irritating cricket injury. He fractured his arm when facing Bill Hitch in the nets even before the first match was played. No one was more upset than the likeable Hitch, who knew all about physical pain from the numerous blows he received when fielding, often with excessive courage, at short leg.

Mac played just once for England at cricket. His international appearances at football numbered half a dozen. He was inordinately

93

proud of the fact that he captained Aston Villa in the FA Cup Final, and stepped up to receive the trophy from the Duke of Gloucester. He loved both codes equally; there were individual deeds, fine, flawless performances, that he had every right to recount with a glow of self-congratulation. He never did. 'It actually drove him bonkers when people came up to him and tried to draw him into a conversation about football or cricket. He would politely start to talk about something else,' says his daughter.

His wife was not besotted with sport. She didn't hoard, in any sentimental sense, many of the mementos of Mac's rich career. Daphne wishes she'd kept more. Her own prized, small collection comprises two international caps and a Cup-winners' medal. She remembers how envious some of her school friends were that she had a quite famous father, particularly when she told them about county cricketers being brought home to supper after the close of play. She regrets that, in the way of children, she was apt to be blasé about his achievements. She never saw him play football, although in the summer holidays he'd take her to some of the cricket festivals, like Weston-super-Mare and Hastings. Then they'd go to the cinema in the evening.

Family life was his greatest joy outside sport. He'd met Vera, or 'V', whose family kept the Holte hotel near the Villa ground, when the players - immensely glamorous figures, as they still are, around the Midlands - used to call in. It was a thoroughly happy marriage. Mac would have walked away from the merest murmur of a family row. He was endearingly hopeless in the house. Wife and daughter smiled and tolerated his ham-fisted disasters. In the end they knocked in the nails and changed the fuse. Daphne was to say years later: 'Mother always carved the joint - it never crossed my mind that men did things like that. Nor was Mac much of a gardener, though he did once scoop out a hole on the lawn so that he could practise his putting.'

He was a warm-hearted and simple man. He liked Laurel and Hardy, and the Crazy Gang. If his Surrey teammates tried out a practical joke on him, he was inclined to experiment at home.

Mac always wanted a daughter rather than a son. He encouraged her as junior tennis player and she met with some modest success. They would go swimming together before breakfast and stop at the baker's on the way home to buy fresh rolls. He was exceptionally fit. The June and July sunshine never left his cheeks; his body remained taut and muscular. At times he was almost obsessed with fitness. He gave up smoking. He developed various fads with his food and was briefly a vegetarian. Such quirkiness amused the family.

He was an above-average golfer and an outstanding table tennis player. At times his wife must have wished he had more interests outside sport. If he had opinions on wider issues of the day, one seldom heard them. 'People would come to the house and stay for a couple of hours. When they left, they would turn to Mum at the door and say what a charming chap Dad was. Yet he would probably not have said more than a couple of words all evening.'

The fact was that, though his feats were a matter of so much public interest and often acclaim, he was naturally shy. One can only guess what he made of the engagingly gregarious lifestyle of the occupants, decidedly thespian, of the big house at Great Enton, where he lived latterly. The place was owned by the American playwright Robert Sherwood, of *Petrified Forest* fame, who was for a time Roosevelt's speechmaker. Also in the house were Vera's sister, Joyce Barbour, one-time child star and then scatty Gaiety Girl before turning into a most successful legitimate actress, and her husband Richard Bird, actor and director in his own right. There was much incestuous theatrical talk, often gossipy and indiscreet. The decibels of anecdotal animation would soar. Joyce and Richard, with their West End intimates who called, liked a drink.

There were also the abstainers, like Vera and Mac. Dr Tony Barbour, now an eminent environmental scientist, is a nephew who once played cricket on the lawn with Mac and, like all the family, patently worshipped him. He pondered the somewhat unlikely professional mix at the big house at Great Enton, not least the drinkers and the non-drinkers. 'It was quite a dichotomy, but they all got on remarkably well together.'

Growing up as he did in Southend, showing much aptitude as a club cricketer, it is surprising that Essex disregarded Mac. Perhaps, like many at the time, they thought his heart belonged to soccer.

Surrey were more encouraging. He joined the staff in 1906 and although the county was laden with famous names and rather too many fine batsmen, Mac contented himself initially scoring runs plentifully for the 2nd X1. By 1909 he was in the Championship side on merit. He passed 1,000 runs and earned his maiden century against capricious and ever convenient Somerset.

In all he hit fifty-two hundreds for Surrey. The manner of their acquisition was just as impressive. Everything about him was unforced proficiency. He scored on both sides of the wicket; he used his feet to the spinners, faced the fast bowlers with an intrepid stillness at the crease. He didn't often wear a cap. The appearance was neat, boyish and agreeable. He may have been a relative newcomer to The Oval but people, including the old fogeys in the members' stand, liked the quiet mature way he conducted himself. As for his batting, it was technically fluent. And, blissfully, it didn't manifest the mannered and flamboyant correctness of one of those cocky young graduates straight from the nets.

Mac was by inclination a forcing batsman. At Surrey he was surrounded by great and illustrious players, starting with Tom Hayward and Jack Hobbs. He could so easily have looked a pigmy in comparison. Very soon the wiseacres at The Oval were nudging each other and saying: 'This young Andrew Ducat isn't just a

—

Wilf Wooller, coming to the end of his 400 matches for Glamorgan, but still as competitive as ever

Siegfried Sassoon (seated fourth from right) with the village team at Heytesbury, before a match with Netheravon. His wife (far right) has brought the family dog. On Sassoon's right are shepherd Sam Dredge and estate gardeners Bill Gearing and Bert Turner (with pads on)

The young Dennis Silk with Siegfried Sassoon

Jack Fingleton, jovial and at times acerbic

A smiling Bill Andrews at his beloved Clarence Park in 1975, his final match. He organised it as part of Somerset's centenary celebrations. (Below) With his son Mark who he hoped would follow in his footsteps as a professional cricketer. Here he puts him right on the forward defensive stroke. Daughter Sara watches intently from behind the stumps

Andy Ducat (right) about to resume his innings with Lt D.A.M.
Rome after lunch at Lord's in 1942. This is a historically tragic
picture: shortly afterwards, the great Surrey batsman collapsed at
the wicket and died

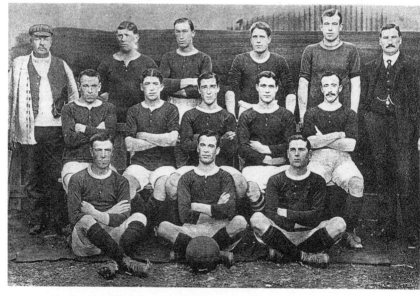

A man for all seasons. Andy Ducat (middle of centre row) in the
Woolwich Arsenal team of 1905-06

*Bill Greswell,
the desperately
frustrated cricketer
and the Home
Guard officer*

Big Jim Smith striding out to bat, ever a joyful Wiltshire slogger

(Below) 'Right, boys, climb into the Rolls - we're off to the Dorchester.' The dashing Bev Lyon with some of the Gloucester- shire team: (back row) E.J.Stephens, Charlie Dacre and Reg Sinfield; (middle) Billy Neale and Charles Barnett. Senior pro Charlie Parker is front left

Bev Lyon, man of vision

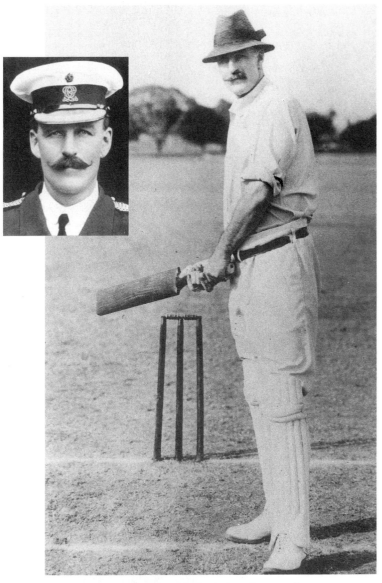

*Robert Montagu Poore worked out his own theories on
batsmanship, including clearly the way he would hold the bat.
(Inset) 'Bertie', the handsome young officer*

Jack Mercer,
mercurial swing bowler
and card ace

The upright Tom
Richardson, one of
England's greatest ever
fast bowlers

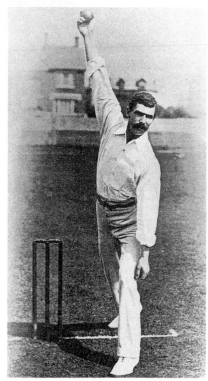

footballer after all.'

It hardly stopped raining in 1910 and runs were elusive around the gloomy circuit. Ducat's 153 against Yorkshire was the best by any Surrey player that summer. He repeatedly put his left foot down the wicket and drove beautifully. Teammates would say: 'Just like Jack out there today, Mac.' He couldn't ask for a greater compliment than that.

That innings against Yorkshire took him less than three hours. First he had Hobbs at his side, then the audacious and vastly entertaining Hitch. It was a demoralising match for the North Country.

Like so many who played professionally at more than one sport, Mac possessed an innate sense of timing. He got into position quickly, not because of what he had been taught by the county coach - though he was an avid listener - but because instinctively it was the natural thing to do.

In the pattern of many attractive fast scorers, he never slogged or seemed in excessive haste. He moved more like a winger than a wing half between the wicket, judging a quick run to perfection. 'You'll be the death of me,' Andy Sandham used to mutter through a half-smile as he puffed past.

The absence of competitive cricket during the First World War hardly retarded Ducat's progress as a first-class batsman. He came back in 1919 and scored 306 against Oxford University - and in those post-war days, Varsity cricket glowed with batting and bowling talent.

The innings was something of a sensation. It took only four hours forty minutes; the first hundred came in two hours, and from then on, Mac treated the Oxford attack as if it was something he used to toy with on a Corporation park back in Southend. At one point, he hit nine fours and a five off successive strokes. Abel, breezing along pleasantly at the other end whenever he could get the strike, simply stood and applauded.

In that 1919 summer, when the Championship games were limited to two days, there were other memorable matches for him. A week before he mutilated the University, he'd scored 190 against Sussex in three and a half hours, and arguably given one chance. Then the next month, down at Southampton, he made 271 with more thoroughly good-looking aggression. That put him into the county's record books for his third-wicket stand of 353 with E.G. Hayes. He is also there, while we are on the subject, for his tenth-wicket partnership of 173 with Sandham in 1921. Don't let's try to work out what happened to the batting order that day.

Test recognition was hard-earned for a batsman in those rich-textured summers. Mac had been one of *Wisden's* Five Cricketers in 1920 and the following year he found himself in the England team against the Australians at Leeds. The selectors reasoned that he could stand up without flinching to fast bowlers as well as anyone in the country at that time. Gregory and McDonald wouldn't frighten him. The pace and poetry of his out-fielding were also seen as a bonus. England had been altogether too sloppy in one or two recent Tests.

If Ducat's untimely death, bat in hand, offered a plaintive piece of cricketing history, his solitary appearance for England provides another strange cameo. A delivery from Ted McDonald reared awkwardly onto the shoulder of Mac's bat. The shoulder splintered in a cruel way never before seen in a meadowland village game, let alone a Test match. The ball flew straight to Gregory in the slips for a catch. To compound the irony, a splinter from the shattered bat dropped onto the wickets and dislodged the bails. Dismissal in duplicate on one's Test debut. The sympathetic wicket-keeper, Carter, handed Ducat the piece of fallen timber. 'Might as well have it as a souvenir,' he said.

The unlucky batsman wasn't chosen again. So he went back to

scoring runs consistently for Surrey. His last hundred, the only one for him that season, was in 1931. By then the county committee had already made the decision not to renew his contract. It was hard to justify their decision: he had compiled 2,000 runs and hit five centuries, including one against MCC only the previous year.

He did his best to mask his disappointment. In the dressing-room with the teammates he fidgeted self-consciously. He had known much personal success; now, privately, he found it hard to accept rejection from a county he had served for a quarter of a century.

Surrey were pretty sheepish about it. They resorted to the age-old standby: they were in a bad way financially and had to save some money. Several poor summers had affected the size of the crowds. So the county were having to reduce the number of 2nd X1 fixtures - and, additionally, would be forced to part company with one or two of the older pros. Mac was in his mid-forties, supposedly on the decline. That meant he was expendable; so was Alan Peach, the popular all-rounder warmly regarded for his fiery batting alongside Percy Fender.

It was probably the biggest disappointment in Ducat's fruitful life. Cricket as conversation was taboo at home but 'V' could tell how much her husband was hurt. He argued that because he'd looked after his body so well, he was good for another season or two in first-class cricket. In fact, the two dejected old pros were to turn to coaching. Peach returned to Surrey as coach from 1935-39, encouraging the emergent Alec and Eric Bedser in the process.

Ducat was to be senior professional coach at Eton for five years. It was an ideal choice: the tuition was imparted with an amiable voice that was never raised or revealed a suggestion of impatience. Everything he did was technically sound. He lifted a yellowing, old bat off the shelf and handled it with the respect a professional musician shows for his violin.

—

When Mac died, Mr C.H. Taylor, the master of cricket at Eton and himself a former Oxford Blue all four years - indeed he was the first Oxford freshman to score a hundred in a Varsity match - was to write in *Wisden*: 'He won the affection of all by the rare qualities of enthusiasm and modesty which he combined with great cricketing skills.'

One would have thought that Ducat was almost too diffident to be a successful coach. Might he have been even too bland, too introverted, too lacking in strong opinion? His wife was to admit to friends and relatives that she was 'astounded' how well he did on a lecture and coaching tour of Australia. 'It was something he had never done before. But he stood up, in front of the students, and chatted away in a completely relaxed and natural way. The thing was he knew his cricket so completely. He liked young people and he enjoyed passing on his experience.'

Clearly he had much charm - and even leadership qualities - beneath that fairly laconic exterior. This was evident when he pulled on the claret and blue shirt, livery of the sporting tradition, to skipper Villa. There were many noisier members of the famous team, many with more strident opinions. His leadership was based on example. He hardly ever had a bad game. Though not a six-footer, like several of his teammates, he had the muscle and stamina to offset the most cloying mud. His reserves of energy were wonderfully demonstrated in the 1920 internationals against Wales and Scotland, staying on his feet, ploughing through the slush in the most challenging of conditions.

Everyone was impressed by his temperament. Never once in his whole career was he in trouble with a referee. His tackling was sharp and incisive, never late or suspect in intent. Colleagues with cruder styles and more bellicose natures were surprised that he refused to retaliate when subjected to malicious challenges. Daphne told me: 'Those who watched him regularly said they didn't once see him commit a foul.'

He won his first three international caps when with Woolwich Arsenal, in 1910. It was as the quiet idol of Villa Park that he achieved his greatest reputation as a polished, unruffled wing half. The FA Cup win at Stamford Bridge was earned agonisingly. Villa were the unquestionable favourites. They had Sam Hardy in goal, and Billy Walker breezing away in the attack. The all-international half-back line was as formidable as anything in the League at that time. Against the predictions, Huddersfield showed no inclination to be impressed by mere reputation. In the end, Villa won in extra-time. The ball went in, following a corner, off the back of Kirton's neck. He didn't even know he'd scored.

We have touched on Mac's paradoxical qualities. No one would ever have imagined him becoming a manager. But that was what happened, briefly, in 1924. He was coming to the end of his soccer career and injury was curtailing his cricket. The Surrey county club weren't enchanted, indeed they were rather cross, when they heard what he was going to do. They could foresee conflict again over the normal pre-season cricket training and future loyalties in the summer. Mac had heard other pros at Villa talking rather grandly of their managerial ambitions. Across Britain, economic depression was lengthening the dole queues. It was quite flattering, and appeared to make practical sense, when Fulham offered him the job of manager. He liked Craven Cottage; it had a nice homely unsophisticated feel about it.

No one is too sure how much he enjoyed the responsibilities. It is doubtful whether he was assertive enough. He was a novice at what was later called man-management. He would never have been able to crack the whip if a dressing-room huddle of cockney footballers had suddenly become petulant or wanted to impose their own will. Home with his family, he seemed rather more preoccupied than usual. One Sunday lunchtime, perhaps when his

—

mind was back at Craven Cottage, he swallowed a chicken bone and had to be rushed to hospital.

Fulham escaped relegation, but only just. Mac decided it wasn't for him. 'Think I'll stick to cricket, without the worries,' he told 'V'. He handed in his resignation as manager but because of restricted newsprint at the time, the news didn't get into the papers straightaway. A newspaper report in May 1926 said, without too much explanation: 'It came as some surprise after the Strike to learn that Andy Ducat's resignation had taken effect. He was expected to stay on.' Ned Liddell succeeded him.

Mac hadn't lived extravagantly. But once his cricket with Surrey had finished, he complimented his earnings as a coach by turning to journalism. He covered football and cricket for the *Daily Sketch*. His judgments showed wisdom, acquired as a player in both games at top club level over thirty years or so. The *Sketch* would probably have liked him to be a little more opinionated at times - but that wasn't his style. He loved this new part-time work; it kept him emotionally in touch with professional sport. He was a popular occupant of the press boxes around the country, London and Home Counties grounds in particular.

His approach to journalism was as efficient and conscientious as that to sport. He set off from home, as his daughter remembers, with a row of freshly sharpened pencils in his breast pocket. He'd always got on well with the reporters. Now he was one of them, a reflection that amused him as he travelled back on the train after an afternoon at Highbury or Lord's.

It rather appealed to him getting into print. He had been invited to do a coaching book in the mid-Thirties, though the publishers, Hutchinson & Co, had employed a ghost to put Mac's thoughts down on paper. The ghost actually got a bit above himself and started writing about 'the immortal Mr Pickwick' and Dingley Dell on the first page. At least by page 56, the author was being allowed to express some genuine views of his own. He was actually advocating the revival of lob bowling. 'Your good lob bowler can make the ball break either way at will, and bring it off the pitch with the true Maurice Tate "nip". Batsmen of Test match class have often been tied down by a lob bowler - the much despised sneak of schoolboy slang.'

Who said Ducat went through life without opinions of his own?

In the wake of the reverberating 1932-33 tour of Australia, he also included a short chapter on bodyline, which he pointed out had - under the guise of leg theory - been practised for years by medium-paced bowlers. 'It was in vogue, of course, before the 1914-18 war. The late A.Jaques, of Hampshire, was a well-known exponent. To give some idea of the prospect of scoring runs on the off-side, I would mention that he had only one fieldsman on that side of the field, at mid-off.'

Mac wrote from experience - and with a smile on his face. At The Oval, he once ran seven off a delivery from Jaques. It was early in the season when the wickets were pitched close to the gasometer side. That left a vast space on the other side of the ground.

The Hampshire bowler had packed his leg field. C.B. Fry was a solitary figure at mid-off. 'Getting one ball a little over-pitched and not swerving as usual, I was lucky enough to cut it to where third man would have been in the ordinary way. The ball looked like reaching the boundary but stopped a yard short. C.B., who even then was by no means slow, had to sprint after the ball . . . we ran seven.'

Ducat scored more than a thousand runs in a season fourteen times. Yet, because of the richness of talent - not to mention the prejudices and whims of those in authority, he played just once for England. Poor Tom Shepherd, the village cricketer who simply made Surrey bring him in after his prodigious hitting for the 2nd X1, didn't even get a sniff of Test recognition.

But just dip at random into the county's scorebooks. What is this: the first four in the order . . . Hobbs, Sandham, Ducat and Shepherd? The psychological cloud weighed heavily on opposing bowlers even before they got to The Oval ground.

In this unashamedly affectionate reassessment of Andy Ducat, I return again to Robertson-Glasgow, most sensitive of souls. This is what he said: 'The character was gentle and kind. Nothing showy, insincere or envious came near to his nature . . . the two things that struck you most were his strength and control. He was beautifully balanced in mind and body.' The marvellous, tragic Crusoe was one of the few to grasp the importance of the mind in all aspects of life, including a cricket match.

There was a big turnout for the funeral. Famous cricketers and footballers went; so did past and present boys and masters from Eton, family friends and members of the Home Guard. Pelham Warner had a kindly word with Vera and her daughter. He arranged for his chauffeur to drive them home to Great Enton. They stopped, Plum and the family, for tea on the way. Daphne thought again of the hot breakfast rolls with her father after swimming.

SIX

BILL GRESWELL

Talent Unfulfilled

———

Greswell, William Territt.

Born Madras, India, 1889.

Died Bicknoller, Somerset, 1971.

Somerset (1908-30, 115

matches); Ceylon (1925-26);

Europeans (1926-27).

An innovative and supremely

gifted medium-pace bowler,

largely lost to English cricket.

BILL GRESWELL WAS THE MOST brilliantly innovative bowler Somerset ever had. His story is also one of the saddest and least known in the county's variegated history.

There is a case for saying he introduced the technique of in-swing bowling to county cricket, though one or two others arguably preceded him or were contemporaries with those unfamiliar, arcane skills. Bill was perhaps the most adept of all, yet at first it never occurred to him that he was doing anything different with the ball or causing consternation among illustrious batsmen.

He had left Repton in 1908 and in five matches for Somerset during the August, he took twenty-two wickets. By the next season, he was earning the grudging admiration of the Australian tourists, finding himself among the most discussed young bowlers in the country. Those who had been inclined to dismiss him as 'just another precocious schoolboy winning premature acclaim' were quickly silenced. The late swerve that he imparted was quite lethal. Wiseacres, sprawled in their canvas chairs in front of the Stragglers Bar at Taunton, stroked leathery faces and said he would walk into the England team.

Greswell in fact played a mere 115 times for his beloved Somerset, never for England. He had a consuming affection for cricket and prodigious, natural gifts as a bowler. He refined these bountiful talents, learning to analyse the curves, diversions and wicked vagaries of his boyishly delivered overs. All he wanted from life was to play cricket. Instead he was sent to Ceylon in work for which he was patently unsuited and he disliked. It must have left him embittered. Yet the public never knew the extent of his anguish.

I remember him as the president of Somerset in the early Sixties. One would find him strolling the boundary, usually on his own. He struck his casual companions as shy. He would watch play with a preoccupied gaze. Now that one knows, it is possible to appreciate the eloquence of his silence: he was still out there, getting the wicket of Hobbs and the others, playing in a golden summer of joy for his county, seeking that elusive fulfilment and all the time doing his best to exclude for ever thoughts of intrusive tea- and rubber-broking. In spirit, he was out there with the Somerset team, trotting in off his few paces and leaving the rest to George Hunt at short leg. The memories were laden with pain and frustration.

Bill Greswell, in old age, cut a lean, gentle figure. He never raised his voice. They said he was probably too diffident to assert firm control on those evenings when as president he took the chair at a tetchy committee meeting. Some of his predecessors had been bristly autocrats, quelling the first signs of rapid fire in the ranks with a rasping, military-style order of unequivocal finality. That wasn't Bill's style. On the surface, he was a compromiser.

Everyone agreed he must have been a fine bowler. 'What a pity you didn't hang around longer in this country. But then, you had a living to think about,' they used to say. He merely shrugged. They probably imagined he made a good deal of money out in Ceylon. 'Most of you chaps did, of course.' Did they? Not in Greswell's case. He may have enjoyed the whisky-and-soda lifestyle, Saturday night dances, and a few of the more privileged activities at the exclusive Princes Club in Colombo, but he accumulated no great wealth. Back in this country, broking in London was less than successful. When he eventually returned to West Somerset, the property was owned by his wife. Indeed, he went through life with relatively few possessions.

There is something strangely, even sadly, paradoxical about the way he chopped logs and grew vegetables to sell at the greengrocers' in Watchet and Williton. He was a rotten businessman. 'He loathed haggling,' his daughter Gill recalled. 'If another price was suggested, he would accept it straightaway. When you took his petrol money into account, he was probably out of pocket on the day's work.'

Sporting life has always been full of paradoxes. Just as Tony Hancock rarely smiled off-stage, so the equally tragic Hughie Gallacher - after whom doting Geordie parents named their children - sparkled only on a football pitch. Nearer to Taunton, did any cricketer epitomise more felicitous humanity than Robertson-Glasgow, or anyone generate more flights of ecstasy through his sublime batsmanship than Harold Gimblett? They represented the highest forms of pleasure and happiness acquired through cricket: and they both killed themselves.

Greswell had been a cricketing hero at school, playing in a marvellous side at Repton which was captained by Harry Altham, who was to become such an influential MCC figure for a quarter of a century and to combine with E.W. Swanton on that formidable and standard work, *The History of Cricket*. His entry to the first-class game had carried a romantic flourish. The other players in the Somerset team liked him, especially the amateurs. But one of the pros, Len Braund, the wily old leg-spinner, fine batsman and one of the West Country's finest slip fielders of all times, immediately savoured what he saw.

'Only one thing wrong with this young feller, Mr Daniell,' he said to Somerset's skipper in that first 1908 season. 'His field needs a bit of changing. He ought to put his slips over on the leg side. That's where the catches are coming.'

And Greswell was to write later: 'That's how my leg-trap started.'

It all seemed to come so easily to the newcomer. At school his assiduous approach had been based on the tenets of the fourth-form manual: Keep a length, bowl straight and NEVER down the leg side. Now that fundamental counsel was being eagerly garnished. To Bill's ingenuous amazement, the ball was swerving through the air without too much conscious effort on his part. It was also moving into the batsman very late indeed. Wicket-keepers, ranging from that solemn amateur Arthur Newton to the earthy professional Harry Chidgey were driven to distraction - and retrospective praise. For the batsmen, many of experience and repute, the experience of survival was altogether more bewildering.

The record books of Somerset illustrate what he achieved in his intermittent career with them. There were his nine wickets in an innings at Weston-super-Mare and, before that, his hundred at Lord's, every bit as eager and brisk as when he batted for fun on the green at Holford, at the foot of the Quantocks, with his friend and near neighbour, Jack White. Bill played for the Gentlemen against the Players. We'll never know what other grandeur in the game he could have acquired.

Most of the county's devotees assumed that he chose to make his living in Ceylon. They discovered that he was to become the finest cricketer on the island and doubtless had leisure time enough to indulge his sporting talents. Future generations in Somerset relied on stray memories and statistics that told no more than a cold, impersonal tale of his deeds. To many, he was a slightly shadowy figure who popped up from time to time in the scorebook. Maybe just another of those supposedly gifted amateurs, of which Somerset had many, who arrived from school in their fancy caps and inevitably went off later to make some money.

What was Bill like? In the year or so he was the county president, I approached him once or twice as a journalist and found him both courteous and taciturn. Members liked his self-effacing manner. Others enjoyed the droll jokes he made to enliven meandering, jejune debates, during his time with Williton Rural District Council. He didn't talk much about his home life.

Neighbours occasionally saw him setting off for his long walks up the rust-earthed hillside that dominated, with its distinctive pastoral beauty, that corner of West Somerset. He was a man who needed his privacy. They liked what they saw. They took for granted that his life was contented and balanced.

The reality was so different. If only they had known.

His domestic life was strained, often riven by tension and conflict. He viewed his so-called business career as a ghastly waste. Some of his family felt he had veiled feelings of guilt about marital and professional failure. He resented the way fate had malevolently, as he saw it, steered him away from a fruitful and maybe exceptional career in county cricket. Back in Somerset, he moped around with too little to do, in introspective moments. The self-induced physical work at least gave him a purpose.

From an old villager, Bill learned the rudiments of gardening. In the summer months he got up just after four a.m. Vegetable and soft fruit-growing became a new passion, something to fill the void. He was inordinately proud of his 1,000 lb of raspberries he picked one year. Against the predictions of the experts, he also proved that he could grow melons. 'Mating' was the problem but where the bees let him down, because they couldn't get under the frames in the sun, he improvised with some ingenuity by using a rabbit's foot tied to a long stick, for transferring the pollen.

But horticulture was only a partial therapy for a restless man with energy to expend. He joined the Home Guard with great enthusiasm in the last war. As commander of the local battalion, he welcomed the responsibilities and administrative duties. There were many stories of unorthodox assignments by the motley assortment of Home Guards in the Quantoxhead area - and authentic reports of rifle practice at the expense of the deer population. Major Greswell relayed with wry humour, a quality of his not always evident, some of the escapades. A practice session with live hand grenades, when Bill was in charge, was perilously near to tragedy. He went to infinite pains to explain to a farm worker from Williton how the pin should be removed and the grenade hurled 'just as if it's a cricket ball'. The instructions were not absorbed and the horrified Home Guard commander bellowed for everyone to fall flat on their stomachs. The grenade went off - and the only casualty was an overweight local grocer whose protruding bottom took the major share of the blast.

Greswell welcomed the chance to be back in uniform, however ill-fitting it was. He had served in the Somerset Light Infantry in the First World War as an officer, and was seconded for a time to the Royal Engineers (Gas Brigade). He was mentioned in despatches for 'gallant and distinguished service in the field' a few days before the end of the war. He'd been sent up to the front line in Northern France on his motorbike, and on his was back had come into a line of fire. As he later described it, with appealing modesty: 'Trying to steer out of trouble, I went straight into the ditch and it probably saved my life. I was really looking after number one and my action was in no way special.'

His previous war service and standing in the local community made him an obvious candidate to command the Home Guard. He carried out his duties with quiet efficiency. His troops, most of them with less time on their hands, were impressed by the sheer energy and enthusiasm he brought to the job.

But then the war was over - and once more there was a fearful emptiness in his life. This led to the second of his serious nervous breakdowns. The first had been in 1931, brought on largely by business failure in the rubber-broking business in London. At Dr Fox's hospital in Brislington, on the outskirts of Bristol, he was one of the guinea pigs for ECT (electro-convulsive therapy). All his life Bill suffered from varying degrees of claustrophobia. This then contentious form of treatment was a thoroughly traumatic experience for him, in the days before the use of anaesthetics in the process. He was strapped down and apprehensive. On one occasion, when he was at the hospital and due for more ECT treatment, he discharged himself.

Much of his life he lacked self-confidence, though significantly this sapping psychological deficiency was never evident when he was playing cricket. A psychiatrist told him more than once: 'You have a dreadful inferiority complex.' Once, visiting the psychiatrist with his second wife, Rachel, the blunt message to the pair of them carried no qualifications. 'You two should never have married - you can't support each other.'

To the public in the West Country he was warmly regarded, a man of gentility. They knew nothing of the blacker side of his nature. His bitterness, which he did his best to hide, manifested itself in oddly teasing actions to domestic pets. His complexes were hard to understand. He was undemonstrative to his children, inclined to greet them with a handshake rather than a kiss. When they were at school, he would write copious letters to them and add illustrations that were well-meaning but had little artistic pretension. Later he was ungenerous in his encouragement to them. He was disappointed that son John was not more of a cricketer. On the morning of the day Gill was due to compete in a gymkhana, Bill took the horse out across the hills and tired it out. That kind of uncharitable action was impossible to fathom. At this distance, significantly, the children's affection for him remains strong.

He was, again in sharp contradiction to those who thought they knew him, a person of deep prejudices. His anti-Semitic attitudes were unbending. 'He had only to see an opulent car going by with GB plates and he'd claim it was being driven by a "Jew boy".' He hated all Labour politicians after the war - 'those bleating sheep of the Left' - and Emanuel Shinwell most of all. The pathological dislike of Shinwell could be almost entirely attributed to his Jewish roots. Bill even had suspicions about Jack Meyer, the Somerset cricketing eccentric and Millfield founder, because of the sound of his name. In fact, RJO's father had been an Anglican canon.

The bigotry extended in a number of directions. He didn't like blacks or Yorkshiremen, which must at least show some sort of spectrum of intolerance. During his time in Ceylon, he was 'quite horrid' about black people, according to his wife. They had three servants at their spacious bungalow home, looking out over the sea, in Colombo. All three walked round the house without shoes. The house-boy infuriated Bill by his little trick, oft-repeated, of wriggling one toe over the next. As the head of the house, Greswell was the unchallenged voice of the old Imperialism.

Yorkshiremen were almost as unattractive to him. He once wrote to Len Hutton with a specific request for a visit to the West Country, and got no reply. Hutton was never forgiven. When in 1970 Brian Close was invited to come to Somerset as captain, Greswell was appalled.

Much nearer home, he never really took to Harold Gimblett, who came from Blake's Farm, just down the road in Bicknoller. Again that bit of parochial prejudice is not easily explained. Could there have been an element of snobbery? Or were the pair, both suffering from gnawing nervous tensions and a dozen intertwined complexes fermenting into paranoia, just too similar?

In the dressing-room, Greswell was coolly friendly rather than convivial. His closest friends were Sammy Woods, with whom he really did tramp the Quantock Hills and stop at the Aussie's bidding to share a few gulps of ale from a hidden bottle (Sammy's concealed brewery bases were more than an after-hours legend), and Farmer White. He had reservations about John Daniell, who he said could be too quirky over team selection and would leave you out on the morning of the match.

William Territt Greswell was born in Cuddalore, Madras, in 1889. His father, Charles, had been out there since 1870, working as an engineer for the Ceylon and Indian railways. That provided no more than an adequate living; it was an era for business speculation among the sizeable number of Brits and though not a risk-taker, he had the foresight and confidence to buy a thousand acres of overgrown jungle in Ceylon. He had it cleared and put down to tea and rubber. It was a profitable exercise: yet only at this distance do we realise the way the balance sheet swayed cruelly, in the psychological sense, against Bill. That cultivated jungle in effect determined the course of his life.

His parents had five children, though one died in infancy and another when aged only eight. That left a brother and a sister for Bill. The brother, Ernest, went on to play a dozen games for Somerset. At Repton there was an occasion when, as part of the public school ritual, Ernest as a prefect had to beat Bill. The younger brother escaped from the study by crawling under a table and running away. He later attributed his action to cowardice. There was no question of resenting the disciplinary strictures of the sibling prefect. The two remained great friends, at times leaning on each other in life. Ernest's death in 1962 was a fearful blow to Bill. He had worked as a forestry officer in India and for the university appointments board in Oxford, and then came back to retire at Bicknoller.

From the day in 1909, when Bill arrived in Ceylon at the behest of his father to manage the estate and gradually to assist the broking operation in Colombo, the schoolboyish brio that characterised his four fruitful years in the 1st X1 at Repton patently drained away. He liked the hot curries, the Saturday dances, the abundant sport; he loathed the work.

In England he had played hockey for the West of England. He

captained hockey and football teams in Ceylon and won the middle-distance races in the occasional athletics meetings. But cricket remained his obsession. Never once did he play, for the best clubs in Ceylon, without fervently wishing it had been Taunton or Bath, or even on the green back at Holford.

His record as a bowler out there was by local standards phenomenal. He was the first European to take one thousand wickets, most of them in what were regarded as senior matches. Several times he captured all ten wickets in an innings. Significantly, well over half of his victims were bowled or went leg-before. It is not documented to what extent he experimented with this Braund-inspired leg trap, or indeed how many catches were put down by inexperienced fingers. In 1911 alone, Greswell took 232 wickets, unquestionably a record for Ceylon in those days. One might reasonably wonder how much time was devoted to tea-planting and office matters.

The illustrious MCC side stopped off in 1920 and 1924 on their way to Australia. They may have been feeling the effects of the sea journey and individual joints may have been stiff. But this could hardly be a valid excuse for their miserable performance, complete humiliation saved only by the diplomatic way that this particular Saturday fixture was called off in the end because of supposed fading light and poor weather. 'We really beat 'em, you know,' Bill would relate years later.

In a letter home to his father in 1920, he wrote:

Their last man was in and they still had 15 or so to make . . . It would never have done for us to beat the All England side. They would have had their legs pulled for the rest of the tour. Personally I have never taken part in such a game. It was a more thrilling finish than the Australian and Somerset match at Bath, when I was playing years ago and we lost by one wicket.

———

The weather was perfect and the wicket a real good one. There was an enormous crowd, fully 8,000 paying for admission. In the afternoon I got the first four men out for about 30 runs. They were a useful bunch - Hobbs, Woolley, Makepeace and Douglas - and I was very pleased with myself. We had all their batsmen completely tied up. Rhodes and Wilson alone made a long stand but scored only 17 runs in an hour. When we drew stumps, the MCC had made 108-9 and we had the match in our hands. Our fielding was simply miraculous. Douglas said he had never seen such fielding in his experience of cricket . . .

The MCC are a very sporting lot and took it very nicely. Douglas repeatedly asked me when I was coming back to England and said I would get into the England side if I did. Very good of him . . .

Bill didn't make much of a success of marriage. His first wife, Doris, was described by relatives as 'a nice enough person, even if she lacked charm'. She quite liked the social life in Ceylon but failed to enthuse in any way about her husband's cricket. They were married in the May of 1914, just before Bill went off to the war. One version was that she proposed - he 'was too weak to say No'. There were two sons, one of whom served with distinction in the Royal Air Force and retired with the rank of air commodore.

Rachel, the second wife, was invited out to stay with the couple in Ceylon. By then the marriage was rocky and she did not contribute to its disintegration. Rachel was a Sadler, a family socially well-established in the Tiverton area. She was part of the county hunting set - and had a mind of her own. They were married in a register office in London. Divorce carried something of a stigma; the blossoming relationship and wedding created quite a stir among relatives and friends. Rachel's mother didn't approve of the marriage at all. There were hints of snobbery, suggestions that Bill wasn't 'quite good enough'.

They had first met at the county ground in Taunton, introduced by Rachel's uncle, Arthur Newton, the slightly supercilious Old Etonian who kept wicket with much ability for his school, Oxford and Somerset. He played just under two hundred games for his county, was known to stand up to Sammy Woods and made his final nominal appearance in a club match at Taunton when into his eighties.

Rachel was lively and good looking, never without a partner in the Hunt Balls of her youth. She revealed her independence of spirit in the self-confident manner in which she went off to stay with a friend in London. Her conventional parents were even more startled when they discovered, initially to their horror, that she had had her hair bobbed. 'I think it was the bravest thing I ever did - maybe some kind of statement,' she told me years later.

Right through their married life, that kind of independent streak added to the domestic tension. At home, Bill never raised his voice, but the regular exchanges could have quite a jagged edge. He became more and more withdrawn, bottling up his resentment over something that had been said. The two children of the marriage, Gill and John, were at times affected by the uneasy mood within the house. 'I remember running away from the breakfast table in tears - and mother coming up to my room to comfort me,' says John. Bill's mother-in-law stayed with them during the war, contributing to the meal-time friction. She 'never forgave him for marrying Rachel'.

Bill's views on marriage appeared to become increasingly jaundiced. When Gill was about to marry David Goodland, later to be appointed senior history master at Clifton College - his father also played for Somerset - her mother asked: 'Are you going to have a double bed?' Bill instantly mumbled, *sotto voce*: 'No such thing.' She was left to ponder that nebulous Freudian statement. There was much evidence that her father 'couldn't handle emotion in the raw', as the children put it. After a television performance of Rattigan's *The Deep Blue Sea*, Gill and John were discussing it with much enthusiasm. Their father didn't approve at all.

'You've a lot to learn,' he snorted.

But their affection for him was considerable. They accepted his whims and the complexes that manifested themselves in oddly cruel, unpredictable actions. They understood his frustrations which at times were almost unbearable for him. He may well have felt he had negligible status in the household. He was lonely and there were certainly occasions when he would have welcomed more visitors to his last two homes, Weacombe and Orchard Combe - though he had loyal friends with whom he could reminisce.

But we must come back to his cricket. He still looked a slim schoolboy when he had his first county match, against Middlesex at Taunton, in the August of 1908. Tarrant, Littlejohn and Wells, the last two bowled, were his opening victims. In his next match, against Hampshire at Southampton, *Wisden* reported: 'When Hants were 243 on, Greswell bowled with such deadly effect as to take 7 wickets for 19 runs.'

In 1909 he was an emergent name of exceptional promise. Everyone agreed; the Test selectors were well aware of his 'new-fangled techniques'. Nor could his batting be ignored. He went off to Lord's and, in an innings befitting the occasion, he scored a hundred. It took him a mere seventy minutes, having gone in at No 9. Brother Ernest played in the same match and there was vast pride in the congratulations that followed the century. Bill also took nine wickets in this fixture at cricket's headquarters.

When it came to playing the Australians at Bath, young

Greswell's temperament was affected. It might have been a form match at Repton. The tourists needed only 66 when they batted a second time. In the end, they scrambled home by two wickets - though one of their players, Whitty, was sick in an hotel bedroom. Greswell's figures were 20.3-7-38-4. He dismissed both openers, McAlister and Carter, then went on to bowl Hartigan and Gregory.

In this low-scoring match, Somerset made 93 and 111. The Australians did little better: 139 and 68 for eight. Just as Greswell was unplayable in the second innings, so had Ernie Robson been in the first (8 for 35). The finish was as taut and thrilling as any match ever played in the West Country. A yorker from Greswell is popularly thought to have skimmed the stumps without taking the bails off. In any case, Laver survived - and the relieved Australians won with a couple of snicks. Somerset's wicket-keeper, the homely Harry Chidgey, was in tears. Monty Noble, the Aussie skipper, said: 'Those two fellers, Robson and young Greswell, should be in your Test team.'

By 1928, Bill was coming up to forty and was home permanently in this country. At Weston-super-Mare, against Hampshire, his marvellous figures were 41.1-20-62-9. The other wicket was taken by his West Somerset friend from boyhood, Jack White; it had been the eighth to fall. George Hunt's ever reliable, artisan hands at short leg and leg slip brought Greswell five catches. Good-natured friends at Clarence Park claimed Bill's nine wickets were a good deal less surprising than Crusoe's 53 in the same match.

Any study of Greswell's intermittent brilliance as a first-class cricketer inevitably focuses, for the game's historians, on his style as a bowler; his curiosity value, if you like. Many were mystified, especially in his earlier days with Somerset, by what he was doing with the ball. A generation of pundits, including some who went into print, got it all wrong.

The family kindly showed me a letter he wrote as late as 1965 - from a hospital bed, in fact - in which he attempted to explain 'my right hand in-swing stuff':

I remember well the allusion in *Wisden* to 'googly-type'. This was in essence quite wrong as I never spun a ball in my life. People were misled to that conclusion because, as the ball left my hand, I turned the hand very slightly from right to left for the purpose of imparting the absolute minimum rotation, so that the air drift from left was deflected with maximum effect off the smooth cover of the ball onto the ridge of the seam which acted as a sail of a ship.

Such a graphic analogy shows the extent of his analysis, even though he was barely conscious of the stir he was creating, among the game's cognoscenti, at the time. His letter goes on:

In the early stages the swerve, taking effect from about halfway, was quite prodigious. I remember bowling one at J.W.H.T. Douglas at Taunton. He advanced his left foot to off-drive me to the covers, spreading his legs for the perfect shot. The ball dipped in late, passed on the *inside* of his left leg and knocked the leg stick so that it slanted towards the square leg umpire . . . My pace was slow medium but I could put down an occasional faster one. All my deliveries were in the nature of cutters. When the ball pitched it followed the 'in' direction at comparatively greater speed. If I found a bit of green top outside the off stump, it was just heaven.

Bill Greswell was something of a tragic figure in the last years of his life. He had always been liked by everyone in sport, and indeed by the local community in the embracing folds of the Quantock Hills. By now Sammy and Farmer White had gone on. His name meant less and less to the successive generation of post-war players at Taunton.

He now spent most of his days in a small, newly built section of the house over the garage at Orchard Combe. He slumped in the armchair, watching television incessantly and often unseeingly. Not too many called to see him. Bill, a religious man, read his Bible, *Lorna Doone* and his book of devotional thoughts over and over again. Mental decline, at first gradual, became far more marked. Life was not easy for Rachel.

Bill Greswell died early in 1971. The parish church at Bicknoller was crowded for the memorial service. Somerset's president, Bunty Longrigg, was there; familiar, bronzed ever-summery faces, like those ex-pros, Bill Andrews and Bill Alley, could be seen in the congregation.

A clerical friend, Prebendary G.E. Tucker, with whom Bill used to go pigeon-shooting years before, wrote the address - as he had promised - but was too ill himself to deliver it. Colin Atkinson, who had just given up the captaincy of the county side and was much admired by Greswell, deputised.

In his excellent tribute to this unfulfilled cricketer, Prebendary Tucker got two things mildly wrong. With a nice, never reprehensible, sense of romance, he dallied on that momentous match with the Aussies in Bath and assured the rapt occupants of the packed pews, transformed in spirit to boundary seats, that it was the very last delivery when Bill hit the stumps and the bails cussedly stayed on.

And, tut-tut, Harry Altham was described, apart from being his captain at Repton, as his life-long friend. That was an opinion Greswell would have found it hard to endorse if he'd been shown the memorial service address in advance. He was convinced that

Altham was the influential MCC committee man who once confided to the Test selectors that Bill was far too young for such elevation. It was, as he saw it, a hurtful lack of school-chum loyalty that rankled for the rest of his life.

SEVEN

JIM SMITH

Big Heart and Biceps

---

*Smith, Cedric Ivan James. Born
Corsham, Wiltshire, 1906.
Died Mellor, Lancashire, 1979.
Middlesex (1934-39, 152
matches).
Tests: 5. MCC tour to West
Indies 1934-35. First-class
debut was for Minor Counties.
Fast bowler, also renowned for
his big hitting.*

JIM SMITH WAS NEVER ANYTHING but a moonraker. Every shot was intended to clear the lofty spire of Salisbury Cathedral. Opposing captains needed more than the rolling acres of the Wiltshire Downs to station distant fielders in vain pursuit of a catch. His voice retained the vowels of Corsham, untouched by the cockney inflections from his days in the nets at Lord's, or the banter of a Blackburn barside.

Corsham, with its Court and honeysuckle cottages, was more of a village in the years when he was growing up there. He remained quintessentially a country lad. When he later lived in Northampton, he had a smallholding adjoining the family house. And so he had, years after, at the back of his pub in Mellor. He kept a few pigs, some hens, geese and one or two turkeys to be fattened up for Christmas.

He was sublimely happy when he went out, this big, shambling man, to feed his animals. If he hadn't been a professional cricketer, he could have ended up a farmer. But, in reality, he'd have probably been persuaded to help full-time his father, Eli, who apart from being a skilled plasterer, was much in demand as a stone roof tiler, who also specialised in ornamental cornices for country houses. Eli, it should be noted, was renowned for the strength of his forearms, a requisite for heavy work on the roof.

Big Jim Smith was above all an entertainer. There is a rough kind of justice in the way we rather too often remember fine bowlers for their unconventional batsmanship. It also happened to Arthur Wellard.

There was nothing remotely amusing about Jim's bowling. It was straight, technically good to look at, and frequently productive. As a batsman, his manual was plucked from a Wiltshire hedgerow. It owed nothing, not even a faint margin-note, to science. He didn't necessarily smile himself, but everyone else did: with the exception of the savaged bowler or maybe a distracted skipper.

———

Those who write about the game's indelible sloggers come at some point to Smithy. His faithful chroniclers all accept that he didn't last for long. There were many failures at the crease. His dynamic innings were rarely more than cameos, punctuation sequences of fallible haymakers that came and went in the time it took the next man to strap a pad.

It was generally agreed that Jim Smith possessed one shot, a monumental heave after his oversized left boot had been ponderously planted somewhere in the direction of mid-wicket. He might, in good humour, have contested the supposed limitations of his repertoire. One contemporary of his from Minor Counties days in Wiltshire was warmly generous. 'Of course he wasn't a good bat. But what an incredible hitter. A sort of Botham of the Twenties and Thirties - with much less skill and style, I have to say. Jim hit on the up and it was mostly into the V. Not a lot ended up round the corner.'

Maybe distance and time lend romance to the memory. Certainly there were many occasions when wicket-keepers put their gloved hands on their waist and waited interminably for the skier to come down. Long legs and even deep third men had their quota of catches from Jim. The hammer blows, mostly emanating it appeared from those yeoman forearms of his, turned geometry on its head. No skipper, however intuitive himself, had any idea how to place a field for him.

The success as a cricketer, talented enough to play for England, came from his bowling. His therapy - and the infinite joy he was apt to give a nation of expectant watchers - arrived when he picked up that heavy bat and made his way, with cumbersome strides, towards the square.

Denis Compton's personalised genius was spawned from within him. There were influences on him in his shy, fledgling days - but they were not numerous. He didn't need too many of them. Yet he always acknowledged the way that Jim Smith instilled in him the values of entertainment. They were at Lord's together in the Thirties. Compton greatly admired the big man's earthy, unassuming manner. He admired even more the way that bars emptied and members chuckled in anticipation whenever Smith was bracing muscles and with a minimum of ceremony putting bowlers of national repute on the level of undistinguished mates back in Melksham and Malmesbury. There was a wreath from Compton at Big Jim's graveside.

The Smiths had always loved their cricket. Eli wasn't much of a player but his brother Jesse was. He played for Corsham and Wiltshire and was probably responsible for giving young Jim the urge to keep clearing the boundary elms. In the history of Corsham CC, covering the first eighty years up to 1928, H.S. Lakeman was to write: 'Jesse Smith proved himself invaluable with bat and ball. On repeated occasions, his leviathan efforts delighted the onlookers. Twice in 1898 he topped the century and throughout he batted with judgment.' Ah well, maybe the doting nephew, born eight years later and fired with family tales of Jesse's feats, was rather less discriminate.

There was at times a strong case for making Corsham the best local side in the county. Apart from Jim Smith, their most famous player was Septimus (Paul) Kinneir, who had more than three hundred matches for Warwickshire. He was a left-hander who went to Australia under Plum Warner in 1911-12 and had one Test. His obituarists were to say that he was one of the finest batsmen ever to play for Warwickshire. His consistency as an opener earned him considerable praise. Not everyone was as enchanted with some of his stodgier innings, or laboured fielding.

He was freer with his strokes in his Corsham salad days. The club had some marvellous seasons, going through without a defeat, causing oppositions to cower. In mid-week matches, as a concession to the other team, they were known to reverse the batting order completely 'to give our opponents a bit more chance'. It wasn't arrogance. Corsham, however formidable their playing strength, were a popular fixture. If anything caused visitors to quake, maybe it was the evocative names of some of the home players . . . Reckless, Tooth, Fido. When Corsham played away, Mr Fido proudly brought out his gleaming, new tricycle - and always gave two of his teammates a lift.

Jim Smith or 'young Jesse' as some of the locals called him, couldn't wait to join this amiable village team. Nor could his brother, Bill, an accomplished all-rounder who played as a pro for Wiltshire in the mid-Thirties. He was six years older than Jim, and a better footballer. So good was he, in fact, that he gave up his cricket to become a professional with Notts County. With them, he experienced both promotion and relegation. The Smiths always knew the way to get life in perspective.

There were signs of feudal life around Wiltshire parishes if you looked for it. Jim wasn't too bothered. He doffed his cap and showed the normal respect of a village boy for his social betters. He was well-mannered, never obsequious - as R.W.V.Robins was to discover.

As a fellow groundstaff boy at Lord's was to tell me: 'Jim didn't have a particularly high regard for "Cock Robin", from whom a remark could be terribly cutting. You could tell what Jim was thinking by his silence and maybe the glance he would shoot at one or two of us. He looked down on Robins literally. There was never a question of being insubordinate or disrespectful - he could make his valid point without that.'

He probably had more time for Colonel Robert William Awdry, CBE, who took something of a paternal interest in the emergent Smith. The Colonel opened for Oxford in the 1904 Varsity match. But his sporting preoccupation was Wiltshire cricket. With his brother, Charles, superseded in turn by his son, Charles Edwin, he was the driving (even intimidating) force behind the county. First it was his batting; then his captaincy, followed by his influence as secretary and treasurer.

His father owned private cricket grounds at Shaw and Lavington. There were country-house matches, renowned for the skills of the guest players and the quality of the port. Colonel Awdry maintained the level of enthusiasm for the game. He was generous with coaching tips, knowingly retailed from erstwhile evenings in the public-school nets. The strokes could be extravagantly correct. Jim eagerly listened - and still heaved with his own rural pragmatism.

He appreciated the interest being taken in him, and the kindly way he was encouraged to pursue his career at Lord's.

'But you've got to watch yer Ps and Qs. He's the Colonel and he don't let you forget it,' Jim would say.

Mr Reggie Forrester, another formidable name within the context of Wiltshire cricket, recalls: 'In one county fixture, Jim got a delivery to bounce up round the batsman's chin. The Colonel went up to him at once and told him not to do that again. I don't suppose it was Jim Smith's fault. Because of his height, he got natural lift. But those were very different days . . . and the Colonel was the Colonel.'

Forrester and Smith, the solicitor and the trainee plasterer: it could be argued that their careers with Wiltshire began together. They played in the same Under-19 county side in 1925. Jim's sister, Dorothy, worked in the Forrester house, first at Chippenham and then at the beautiful Royal Crescent, in Bath.

'Some argued that his brother, Bill, was a better bowler. I didn't. Jim would open with the new ball for Wiltshire before making way for Bill. But we made sure Jim was kept fresh - to polish off the 9, 10, Jack . . .'

Despite his acclaim as a county cricketer and profitable afternoons in the Caribbean sun, a strong case could be made out that his happiest days of all were in the cricketing meadows of the moonrakers. He liked a half of farmhouse cider. He already had a discerning eye for a pretty girl - 'with Dr Wood's maid, Kitty' among his favoured company. And he liked, equally, knocking stumps out of the ground, and losing cricket balls in the adjoining fields of milk thistles.

He had a superb physique, the best in the Minor Counties. In 1930, 32, and 33 he was taking fifty wickets for Wiltshire. Some felt his cavalier attitude to instruction, when it came to his batting, was a trifle more worrying. At the Bemerton, Salisbury, ground in 1933, the county were rash enough to send him in as nightwatchman.

'Nothing silly, Jim. Just stay there till the morning - and then you can have a real thrash. We don't want to lose any more wickets tonight.'

Maybe he was just hard of hearing. In half an hour he scored 82. It was his highest for Wiltshire. Nightwatchmen, once a metaphor for unrelenting caution, took on a new, audacious meaning. The fact was he really knew only one way to bat. There was a wondrous surfeit of outrageous, untimely, illogical and joyful adventure in his career.

That was his final summer for Wiltshire. The county ended second in the table - a position determined after an embarrassing 'recount' and a few disapproving side glances in the direction of Yorkshire. Mr Forrester, who was by then honorary secretary of Wiltshire, attended the relevant meetings. His legal background was possibly of value to him as, doubtless a bemused observer, he listened to the explanations.

Wisden put it pretty succinctly:

An unfortunate oversight in the notifications of the result of a match between Yorkshire 2nd XI and Staffordshire in the Minor

Counties' competition led to a serious blunder coming to light. As originally made up, the final table of results showed Norfolk with 72% top and Yorkshire with 71.66% as 2nd. Some weeks later it was discovered that certain of the columns of figures did not agree. Mistakes had occurred in calculating the points of Yorks and Staffs.

Yorkshire's points were reduced to 68.33 and they were placed 3rd. Wiltshire were 2nd with a percentage of 70.00. At the AGM of Minor Counties Association at Lord's in December, it was agreed that the championship of 1933 should be recorded as "not decided".

It was a thoroughly unhappy business. The fact was that Yorkshire had sent 'a late and ambiguous' report to the Secretary of the Minor Counties, and as a result that county had been credited with the points for a win in a one-day match instead of those for a win on first innings. Inevitably a few innuendoes were flying around; these in turn were met with resentment and some self-righteousness. At least, once the splutters of committee members and counties who felt they'd been wronged had died down, Wiltshire found themselves as runners-up.

'Not a bad way to go out, Big Jim,' his teammates said. They knew they would miss him in 1934 but wished him well as he headed for Middlesex.

'Don't know what I'm letting meself in for. You can always have me back,' he joked. If not Wiltshire, there was surely Corsham, he told himself . . .

In fact, when he did return to his beloved West Country it was usually to visit his family and old school mates, or to play in a special charity or benefit match. There was also that rather bizarre fixture at Stinchcombe - but it isn't easy to be certain into which sporting category that one can be placed.

———

Stinchcombe has long been a rural home, nestling beneath the Cotswolds, of good local cricket in Gloucestershire. Many county players turned out at some time or other on its picturesque and immaculately tended square. Bev Lyon was especially fond of it. That was how he came to organise a two-day match there against a formidable team compiled by Sir Julien Cahn, around whom there were as many stories woven as runs made by the illustrious batsmen he recruited for his special, well-lubricated matches.

Sir Julien, whose furniture business made him a fortune ('Bit out of thy class, Tom, with yer carpets and cheap armchairs down in Barton Street,' the Gloucesteshire players would say teasingly to Goddard), had two magnificent grounds of his own before the Second World War. He grandly took his teams around the world, basked in the aura of celebrity and only complained when his guests revealed a marked tendency to quench their thirst too well at his expense.

'How about it then, Julien. I'll challenge you to a match at Stinchcombe. With a suitable side-bet, of course.'

It was quite an occasion, well publicised. No one was quite sure how much was at stake, but it was surely enough to spice the encounter for two captains never noticeably inhibited about putting their well-manicured hands towards reassuringly bulky wallets. There was no stinting on Bev's part. He persuaded Frank Chester to be one of the umpires; he borrowed official covers from the county ground in Bristol. Village spectators' eyes popped out as they saw Sir Julien's valet helping him on with his pads.

Sitting on the boundary was Andy Wilson, who a season or so before had arrived in a snowstorm from Lord's to begin his new career as Gloucestershire's wicket-keeper. His first home in the West Country was to be at Stinchcombe. He'd started out as a left-arm spinner, even as an amateur outside left for Queen's Park Rangers. But before long, with his new county, he was proving himself both one of the smallest and best stumpers in the county's history - and figuring in the odd record-breaking stand with Wally Hammond, to augment his value to Gloucestershire.

For that match against the selectorial wiles of Cahn, Bev had brought in one of his Bristol chums, a fine wicket-keeper called Ken Harvey, who hadn't the time or inclination for county cricket, in place of Wilson. Unassuming as ever, Andy reflected that Harvey was probably a better player. He bore no grievance and settled down to watch a two-day event that had all the characteristics of a true contest.

'And what a match it turned out to be,' chuckled Wilson. Sir Julien was full of praise for the ground which he said reminded him of one or two in the West Indies where there were also hills as a backdrop. But he was apparently less pleased about the way the covers were used after the first day's play.'

He took a long, hard look at the pitch, complained that Frank Chester hadn't been consulted about the covers around the footholds and implied his team would be at a disadvantage. As far as he was concerned, the original challenge was off. So, one assumes, was the substantial bet. A one-day game was arranged instead. Jim Smith and the other pros, on both sides, weren't concerned. They enjoyed themselves - and were well looked after.

Big Jim had gone on playing for Wiltshire while on the Lord's groundstaff. Indeed he'd made his first-class debut in 1930 for Minor Counties against Lancashire and played ten times for the MCC in first-class fixtures between 1931-33. It was there at Lord's on the groundstaff that he met Wilson for the first time. There may have been a slightly comical contrast in their size but they got on well together. Smith was not wholly enamoured with the oppressive metropolitan milieu of bricks and mortar. He liked to escape to the nets, or to gaze at head groundsman Harry White's cottage. At times he offered to feed the Rhode Island Reds; it reminded him of home. Occasionally he helped in Harry's kitchen garden.

Part of the duties of the groundstaff lads was to bowl in the nets to the sons and grandsons of MCC members. Jim and the others only snatched their own practice in the morning and then in the evenings when the nets were free. Andy saw him as 'a man mountain', rather like another friend, Bill Bowes, maybe a trifle intimidating to some of the youngsters, yet basically so gentle and kindly with his advice. Jim would trundle away for the boys at slow-medium pace: and then, like most of the groundstaff, would become a little faster and more challenging when he felt the pupils had been in long enough.

Harry White tended his little kitchen garden with almost as much care and affection as he bestowed on the sacred twenty-two yards. He exchanged snatches of country lore with Smith. Maybe because Jim liked to give a hand feeding the hens, the head groundsman would pass on valuable bowling tips.

George Fenner may only have played twice for Kent but he proved a conscientious coach at Middlesex. He didn't attempt to change things or curb natural talents. He was wise enough to let emergent prospects get on with it in their own way, with minimal and tactful words in the ear when techniques needed refining.

'He used to hit the ball halfway across the Nursery ground for the lads to catch,' Wilson recalls. 'One day he asked Jim to hit some similar catches. His first sailed right out of the ground into the road. It was so incredibly effortless - and I often thought of that again when he belted his sixes off the Gloucestershire bowlers.'

The fact was that Big Jim just kept clearing the boundary,without really trying. If Percy Fender and Reg Sinfield suffered, they were two of many. Some of the best bowlers of his day acquired the understandable knack of not catching their skipper's eye when he needed them to attempt to curb the Middlesex slogger's latest *tour de force*.

Smith was blissfully not tainted by sophistication. He loved the worldly bonuses that county cricket brought him: the restaurants in the big hotels where the team sometimes stayed, rather more the recommended board-and-lodgings where he and the other young pros were able to stay and so save a bob or two on expenses. He had a big appetite and would polish off the remnants of a substantial fried breakfast on a teammate's plate. He was always happier in a side-street pub than in the cocktail bar of a hotel. The accent broadened as the strong ale coursed its way down. He was a player everyone liked; you couldn't say that about all the professionals around at the time. Certainly not all the amateurs.

In virtually no time at all, he was more than worth his place in the Middlesex side. His first season brought him exceptional success - and 172 wickets, an average of 18.88. He came sixth in the national averages. To his astonishment he was quickly on his way to the West Indies under Bob Wyatt. He played in all four Tests, making his debut in Barbados at the same time as the Warwickshire pair, Eric Hollies and George Paine, Jack Iddon and E.R.T. Holmes.

For this amenable Wiltshireman, the tour was a cultural revelation and something to be savoured. The stories kept him going in later years as he served the drinks, or on those wet afternoons when the league cricketers were forced to huddle in the pavilion. Jim liked the West Indies, the rum punch, the carefree attitudes. He was also rather partial, if startled, at some of Wyatt's bold theories in search of a result.

'He not only had me opening the bowling with Ken Farnes in me opening Test but, blow me, I found meself going in first with Ken as a batsman in the second innings.'

That was a bold ruse. In fact, Smith failed to score in the match, but England won the Test by four wickets. He had every reason to be immensely pleased with his 5 for 16.

Bob Wyatt wasn't averse to a gamble. At Georgetown, in the third Test, Smith batted at No 3 and 5. That was hardly the accepted station for a towering newcomer to county cricket whose main merit was his pace bowling and whose batting predilections found grudging approval from the higher echelons at Lord's. 'Just look what he did with Wally,' Wyatt said in reasoned justification.

It had happened in the second match of the tour, one against Barbados. England were keen for some batting practice and thundered to 601. Hammond was quite magnificent, scoring 281. Smith came in to join him as last man. The pair added 122 in three-quarters of an hour. Big Jim not only lived with the maestro, he dared to outscore him. *Wisden* even opined that he 'overshadowed his partner' in reaching 83. One can only wonder mischievously what Hammond made of this late-innings levity, which was very much to the liking of the local spectators. In the mid-Thirties, though, Wally was still one of the boys. The remoteness, the complexes, the less than generous aspect to his persona had not noticeably surfaced.

That tendency of Wyatt's to turn the batting order on its head reminded Big Jim of what his beloved Corsham used to do, in their case out of sympathy for a weaker opposition, in those mid-week fixtures with neighbouring parishes.

Years later, Wyatt wrote to a cricket devotee in the West Country: 'Jim could make the ball swing late but was unable to get too much movement in the West Indies . . . I remember in one match when he was batting, he connected and drove a skimmer into a tree outside the ground. There must have been fifty spectators up in the tree and they all came tumbling out when the branch broke . . .'

Wyatt may have been prepared to reveal a gambling instinct by promoting the prodigious hitter in the order. But he also reckoned that, in the context of county captain, he knew the way to make him completely ineffective. 'Whenever Smith played against Warwickshire, I instructed my bowlers to aim yorkers at his leg stump. The result was that he was only able to hit along the ground for singles.'

Smith played in one more Test, against New Zealand at Old Trafford in 1937. He opened the bowling with debutant Arthur Wellard. For the student of sporting ironies, the pairing of these two fine county bowlers - the domestic game's two most muscular hitters - offered tangential conversational jollity between overs.

Up to the war, six summers, he took 676 wickets for Middlesex and 795 in all matches. Only in 1939 did he fail to reach one hundred wickets, and then was just four short. At his distance we can contemplate and even wonder at the dramatic impact of his entry to the first-class game: the manner of his consistent hauls in that opening 1934 season, selection for the Players against the Gentlemen and the elevation, almost in the same sweeping movement, to Test match status.

As a fast bowler, who because of his sheer size must have appeared quite intimidating as he approached the wicket on his heavy-footed run-up, never once was he less than honourable in intent as he unleashed the ball. The relayed accounts of bodyline, some of them graphically embroidered, troubled him. Once when Middlesex were playing Gloucestershire at Lord's Edrich got a little exasperated at the obdurate way Andy Wilson, himself a Middlesex exile, was standing up to him.

'I was about 60 and Bill started letting go a few nasty short ones. It didn't please Jim Smith and I heard him tell Edrich to cut it out,' said Wilson. The Gloucestershire man went on to score a hundred. Smith, his former friend on the Lord's groundstaff, was one of the first to congratulate him.

Jim's two sons, David and Peter, were both talented cricketers. They were encouraged by their father, who put up a net at the back of his pub in Lancashire. They used a concrete wicket and he spent some time coaching them. Peter was a quick bowler 'with a lovely action' but he didn't persevere to the same extent as David, a slow left-arm spinner who played league cricket for East Lancashire as an amateur.

That was Jim's club in the Lancashire League immediately after the war. In no time he was a celebrity; his crude batting style, shorn of the merest aesthetic pretension, stimulated chuckles and won games. The war had cut short his county career, but there was plenty of classy fastish bowling left in him. 'He was especially loved by the kids because of this approach,' David told me. 'I went along as his baggage-man, always proud of his feats. How well I remember the ball disappearing into the adjoining tennis courts and bowling green - and even into the grounds of the nearby grammar school. Once when Dad was playing at Rawtenstall, he hammered a ball back high over the bowler's head. It went not only beyond the first row of houses outside the ground but the second row, too.'

When he became landlord of the Millstone Hotel at Mellor, Jim joined Blackburn Northern as an amateur in the Ribblesdale League. Then he returned to East Lancashire, this time also as an amateur.

His weight had always been a matter for good-natured discussion. In his Middlesex days it was fourteen and a half stone going on sixteen. Now it was nineteen. The approach to the wicket had been wisely curbed; the fielding had increasingly been geared to a conservation of energy and movement. The heart - and the felicitous heaves - were still there. So was the slow village-boy grin.

Then, a victim of bad coordination, he stumbled and fell when coming up to bowl. It took four to carry him off. He'd broken his ankle. 'That's it, then. Better stay home and polish the glasses on a Saturday afternoon . . .'

In fact, he found the time to coach for ten years at Stonyhurst College in the Ribble Valley. He patted his big countryman's tummy and looked down on the successive intakes of boys with an innate gentility and helpfulness that characterised his patience and those stage-managed half volleys for the gentry's grandchildren back at the Lord's nets. Big Jim's name is still mentioned with much affection at Stonyhurst.

He retired from the pub at the age of sixty-five - after twenty-two years of contented customers and innumerable cricketing stories at the Millstone. Often his contemporaries from the county circuit had made lengthy detours for the pleasure of calling on him for a chat and shared drink. His nature never really changed.

Throughout his career he enlivened countless grey afternoons, brought bowlers close to tears, damaged bedroom windows and threatened encroaching livestock too oblivious to the wantonly propelled missiles.

At Maidstone he took fourteen minutes over his half-century: and knocked three minutes off when he turned up at Bristol in 1938. That was also the summer when he walked in with a quarter of an hour or so to go at Lord's against Sussex. By the close he'd clobbered 68. Jim Parks and Charlie Oakes grimaced and suffered in comparative silence.

No one surely begrudged Big Jim his only hundred. It came at Canterbury, where the old tree was inevitably battered and must have viewed itself as an endangered species. Ian Peebles, his skipper and last-wicket partner, has written amusingly of this classic occasion. They put on 116 runs between them; of these, Smith bludgeoned 97. He was on four when Peebles came in.

'Not at me best, Mr Peebles,' he confessed later. The innings had taken him 81 minutes. 'Good enough for me, Jim,' said his captain. The St Lawrence ground can be a poet's dream. But it also possesses a certain hauteur. On that August day, not long before Chamberlain's fateful message to the nation, the Kent members rose to applaud Jim Smith off the field.

It was in effect a warm-hearted farewell to a county cricketer who had, blissfully unmindful of the game's rich and graceful technical textures, perhaps entertained the occupants of the boundary seats throughout the late Thirties with his weighty, unsubtle bat as much as any player in this country.

EIGHT

BEV LYON

Visionary with the Yellow Rolls-Royce

———

Lyon, Beverley Hamilton.
Born Caterham, Surrey, 1902.
Died Balcombe, Sussex, 1970. Hard-
hitting middle order batsman.
Gloucestershire (1921-47, 238
matches); Oxford University
(1922-23, blue both years).
Captained Gloucestershire 1929-34,
at times with controversy.

BEVERLEY HAMILTON LYON WAS one of cricket's great visionaries. He could be preposterous and knew no other way to live than to be daring in the pursuit of entertainment. His affection for the game was never inhibited by stodgy convention. He ruffled hierarchical feathers and chuckled to himself as he did it. Only the blinkered elder statesmen, prepared to risk nothing that appeared to take a radical tilt at the monolithic aspects of Lord's, failed to see that he was both a philosopher and a man of ineffable good nature.

He was also the finest captain Gloucestershire ever had. That view was and remains unchallenged - through every sporting back street of Bristol and Cheltenham and across the wide, tumbling contours of the Cotswolds. It comes from those who dotingly played at his side or watched from a boundary bench. But others who only read about him or heard secondhand of his tactical whims and unfettered imagination are just as vehement in their acclaim.

Some argue that he should have led England, too. He'd have done it with a cavalier spirit, full of elan and contentious notions. There would have been much tut-tutting from the loftier bastions of our domestic game. Bill Woodfull certainly wouldn't have known what to make of him: not if, as he was apt to do, he spent the walk to the wicket preceding the toss ruminating aloud with much enthusiasm about the *haute cuisine* he had experienced the night before at the restaurant of his choice. Woodfull's attitude to lavishly sauced meat dishes is not documented, but doubtless he would have preferred to ponder the advantages or otherwise of batting first.

No one in authority would have gambled on Lyon's leadership qualities at the highest level. They had Percy Chapman first to call on, and then Bob Wyatt. By comparison, the breezy and blasphemous Bev simply wasn't establishment material. He was a cricketing 'lightweight', a joker, a populist amateur, the darling of those newspapermen who wrapped their laconic prose round a provocative headline.

How little they knew him. How miserably they failed to recognise his degree of perspicacity under the jauntily angled trilby with its brim bent upwards over the right eye. In fact, he would never have had enough spare time from his business commitments with Rediffusion to go on tour. They weren't to know that.

We can only playfully contemplate what he might have dreamed up for the Aussies in 1932-33. His idea of leg-theory was to station himself at short-square for Tom Goddard. He'd already persuaded big, lugubrious Tom to forget all about medium pace and to go off to Lord's to learn the arcane machinations of off-spin. Now Lyon and Hammond, switched from slip, plucked the dolly catches with a grin on their faces. A grin on Bev's at least. As a skipper, he worked on hunches rather than deep-laid tactical ploys. He couldn't have operated on the combative calculations of a Jardine, though he'd have relished Larwood and Voce on his side (Hammond hated bowling and there was never enough pace to summon up at Gloucestershire).

Lyon's intimates are convinced, however, that he was a strong candidate for the England captaincy in 1934. They still cite the opening Test against the Australians at Trent Bridge. Wyatt had broken his thumb and this placed the selectors in a quandary. They surveyed the list of players and realised that the three fit amateurs had modest or wayward claims. The handsome, young Farnes was, as a fast bowler, in no real position to handle a Test attack. His inexperience also went against him. And Pataudi was, well, an Indian. That left C.F. Walters, who was both the secretary and captain of Worcestershire and had taken a hundred off the Indians a few months earlier. There was a case for bringing in Lyon, who two years running had so nearly led his county to their first Championship title since Grace's day. His rapport with awkward pros was secretly envied by other captains. The higher echelons were always suspicious of such democratic traits; the professionals still had to know their place. And that shouldn't be, as happened at times down in the West Country, in the back of Bev's Rolls-Royce. To his surprise, Walters, a Welshman who could flourish a good-looking bat at the top of the order, got the job. It was his first Test against the Australians and it asked an excessive amount from him.

When the occasional sycophant, at the county ground in Bristol, told Lyon that he had no rival as a captain and was just the man England needed to give them a new resolve and sense of adventure, he laughed and said he had never harboured such grandiose ambitions. Yet he was the most flamboyant cricketer of his day. He was a snazzy dresser, a theatre- and party-goer. He had no coy ideas about self-publicity. If he had something startling to say at a cricket dinner, he alerted his friends in the press. But no one would ever call him a conceited man.

He didn't have much time for cricket's fuddy-duddies. He shocked them because he thought they needed to be shocked. His impish sense of humour - and mischief - left reactionaries quivering with rage in his wake. 'That bloody Lyon is at it again. Says anything to get his name in the papers. Not quite our type . . .'

Anti-semitic feelings were manifested in many sporting corners, not just the golf clubs. A contemporary said: 'We all assumed Bev was Jewish. There weren't many of them around in the first-class game at that time. It was never openly mentioned but you'd hear murmured remarks at social gatherings - to do with Bev's business acumen and the way his brain was always ticking over.' There was a sort of nudge-nudge nuance about the way it was said.

Percy Fender was widely believed - wrongly it appears in his case - to have been Jewish. That was one of the reasons suggested for him not being given the England captaincy. Jewish or not, his tactical battles with Lyon, bubbling mental ingenuity, took on an added piquancy. There is some evidence that Bev came out on top.

That would have led to shared claret, never the merest hint of gloating.

They were two of a kind. Rebellious, cussed, scornful of what others might think of them. They were sharp, intelligent men, competitive by nature. Both had the stray chip on the shoulder, though Bev obscured his better. They abhorred the occupation of the crease for anything but scoring runs, preferably as quickly as possible within the mood and demands of the match. They passionately believed the public had a right to be enthralled by what was happening out on the square.

Just as Fender was apt to speak his mind to the consternation of those who ruled the game, so was Lyon. For years before he was appointed skipper of Gloucestershire, he'd been telling everyone - in the London club, the village pub and the dressing-room - that things would have to change drastically if first-class cricket were to survive.

By 1930 he was advocating Sunday matches. He was saying it publicly in Bristol, 'the city of churches'. Here was real mischief-making. He was a fine orator and his words rang out with sacrilegious fervour. The bishops of the west were horrified. A few ashen-faced clergy climbed the steps of their pulpits to condemn such wanton ideas.

Then, on 11 March 1932 (dwell on that now distant date), he made his famous and much quoted speech at the annual dinner of Gloucestershire County Cricket Club. As captain he was responding to the main toast. His appearance, in his new double-breasted suit, was as impeccable as ever. He had a captive audience and the extrovert in him was in full, positive flow. He wore his glasses but needed rarely to look down on his sparse notes.

'Three weeks ago I had my tonsils out because my doctor told me that as long as I kept them in I should swallow poison day and night,' he began, gaining everyone's attention with such graphic medical detail. 'Yet when I tell you that cricket must have its tonsils out, you'll think I'm being absurd . . .' A trifle tenuous, maybe, rather than absurd.

Bev, the ready joker, was in no mood for laughter. He looked over his glasses at his large company of fellow dinner guests. He reminded them that Gloucestershire had just announced losses of £1,156 and listed the depressing news from other counties. With the only flicker of a smile in his whole speech, he said that Kent had been one of the few lucky ones - they'd made a profit of £23!

What he went on to say is quite remarkable in the light of the game's radical restructuring over the more recent years:

If we had a little common sense we would realise by this time that the weather isn't always fine in England in the summer, and we should make our arrangements accordingly. Of course, there are people who abhor the fact that such a great and wonderful game should become a slave of finance. I agree with them. What fun it would be if we could play first-class cricket without having to worry as to how many people were going to pay a shilling to watch. The hard facts are that to run a first class side costs a good deal of money and eighty per cent has to be taken at the gate. Consequently, something has to go on inside the gate, of enough interest and excitement to attract the crowds.

That's the catch. The young man or woman can now spend a shilling watching dirt-track racing or greyhounds tearing round bends, or gangster films by the hundred. That is the type of crowd we have to attract today.

There are certain rightly respected and very eminent gentlemen who don't understand the changes that have come about in the last fifty years. But then why should they? Would Bach, Beethoven or Chopin understand Jack Payne?

The policy of sitting still and waiting like Mr Micawber for something to turn up seems to me to lack both courage and practicality. The spacious times of the Edwardian era have gone for ever. Lord Hawke can afford to be haughty - cricket cannot. Lord Hawke fiddles while Rome burns.

I am not prepared to stand by while the game I love dies an unnatural death through lack of support. And I believe there is a great volume of similar opinion throughout the country. There is clearly only one thing to try - the clock must come into the game more. Who can deny that cricket is at its glorious best when time is a factor? Allow a batting side three hours only in which to get their runs. And I challenge anybody to tell me how you have spoilt the first-class game. In that way, you get a decision from twelve hours of cricket. If there has been rain, well then six hours' play will give you a decision.

Why can't we have a knock-out competition on these lines, the final to be played at Lord's or The Oval? Let the profits be equally divided among competing counties . . .

There was plenty of applause as he sat down. Those digs at Lord Hawke didn't please everyone. But Bev was Bev: full of far-fetched dreams that he regularly dispensed to anyone who would listen. The Gloucestershire committee knew he was a marvellous captain, who placated weary, grumbling old pros and conjured winning results out of virtually nothing. They indulged him, allowing him his pipe-dreams. And as they cast their plaintive eyes over the balance sheets, they accepted rather grudgingly that one day things would have to change - if not quite in the revolutionary manner Lyon predicted.

'Tis never goin' to happen in our lifetime, skip.'

'It's got to, Charlie, or we'll go under. Let's give it a go, anyway.'

And they did, at the end of April in their final trial match. Stinchcombe Stragglers have a long, affectionate link with the county club. As usual in 1932 there were influential men in those village fields high above the Severn. The Stragglers were captained by Major M.F.S. Jewell, who had recently led Worcestershire. Their team included, for some reason, the redoubtable Essex pair, Jack O'Connor and Laurie Eastman, and forty-six-year-old Alf Dipper, switching sides for the day in his last season for Gloucestershire.

The experimental change of rules for the match, emanating from Lyon's fighting talk at the annual dinner, were well advertised in the local press. This time-limited match attracted three thousand spectators to the village ground. There was a crash-bang innings of 75 by O'Connor for the Stragglers and one of 53 by Lyon himself for the county, who scored 195 and lost by seven runs. It was entertaining stuff, surprisingly not to everyone's liking.

The *Bristol Evening Post* reported: 'We all want brighter cricket, but on this occasion too high a price was paid to secure it. The match produced an exciting finish but the value of the game was reduced as a test of what is a drastic innovation . . .'

Bev had led by example as he aimed his blows for the Berkeley Vale. But too many of the first-class cricketers had been unable to adapt. One day they would have to - and Lyon knew it.

He was disappointed in the muted enthusiasm of that West Country cricket writer. Most of the publicity had been encouraging, however. His flair for publicity had helped; some of the spectators had arrived by air, using a special improvised landing stage alongside the ground.

Bev was born in Surrey, the son of Jeremiah Lyon, a financier who also liked his cricket. Jeremiah was the spectator at Clarence Park, Weston-super-Mare, it emerged many years later, who rushed like a schoolboy onto the pitch and gave Ernie Robson a cheque for £50 after the taciturn all-rounder won a game against Middlesex with a six in the last over.

There were two sons. Bev's older brother, Malcolm Douglas

(Dar) Lyon played with distinction for Somerset and should have been recognised by England. He was the better looking one, while lacking in Bev's effervescent, even overpowering, personality. Both were arguably injudicious in love. Dar walked off with fellow amateur Guy Earle's wife, a marital scandal that would have made the Mendips rumble if it had become public knowledge. Old Jeremiah Lyon, much concerned with matters of propriety, hurried down to see the Somerset secretary, John Daniell, to determine the best way to disguise such carnal indiscretions. As for Bev, he was much embarrassed the way the newspapers went to town on his divorce, an undefended suit, in the spring of 1931. But he liked women, especially if they were striking and blonde. His most constant companion, as the gossip writers still call it, was both.

The brothers' relationship could be, for all their chummy exchanges, quite abrasive. They were very different creatures. Bev was a businessman (let no snob call Rediffusion 'trade'); Dar was called to the Bar in 1925 and later became resident magistrate in Kenya and then Chief Justice in the Seychelles. As boys they played cricket on the lawn together. Afterwards they moved in different directions. A wary competitiveness was never lost. How could it be when one played for Gloucestershire and the other Somerset?

Bev went to Oxford, after doing well as a schoolboy cricketer at Rugby. His form in the 1922 Varsity match was an abject disaster. He failed to score in either innings. It didn't help that Dar was keeping wicket for Cambridge.

Whenever they opposed each other in a county match, one saw little evidence of sibling sentimentality. Some who played alongside them claimed the brothers bared their teeth, metaphorically we assume. On the day Dar made a beautiful 210 against Gloucestershire at Taunton, Bev led the applause. Yet he found it hard to forgive Goddard who fumbled a simple catch in those massive fists at mid-off when the batsman had scored very few.

Reg Sinfield used to tell me of Bev's added resolve when it came to the fixtures with Somerset. His account of that particular match at Taunton is deliciously tinged with ironies. Somerset should have walked it after Dar's wristy double century, compiled in no more than three and a half hours. Bev, altogether less elegant in style, reached his own, single-minded hundred in front of the Bank Holiday crowd. But it was Sinfield, with his long chin and boxer's nose, who brought Gloucestershire the unlikeliest of eight-wicket wins.

'I've got only one instruction for you, Reg. Just stay out there,' said his captain to the one-time cadet and leading hand on C.B. Fry's *Mercury*. No one had a greater sense of self-discipline than Sinfield; no one could be more obdurate if necessary.

'As soon as I got to the wicket I turned to the umpire and said I was sorry about it but I'd be around until half past six. I simply nailed my studs to the ground. The Bank Holiday crowd hated me for it. When they barracked me, I shouted back at them. I'd been told what I had to do.'

He did it with unwavering phlegm for six hours and twenty minutes. It was painfully dreary as Reg, the sweetest natured of men, crawled to his own century. The runs came in prods and deflections: and gradually the initiative was wrested from Somerset.

At the end, Dar glared at his brother. 'If I'd been watching that rubbish, I would have wanted my money back. And you call yourself an advocate of brighter cricket? That was disgraceful, Beverley.'

The younger brother offered a wry smile. 'You took too much for granted. In the end we out-manoeuvred you.' There was immense satisfaction in his voice. The taunts of partial spectators never bothered him.

What did trouble him far more was any social injustice meted out to his players or the merest whimper of a discordant note in the dressing-room. He didn't acknowledge the demarcation line between amateur and pro. There was the famous Long Room incident at Lord's. He arranged for the whole team, whatever the status, to meet in the Long Room so that they could proudly walk out together through the same gate. It was a defiant conflict with protocol and tradition at Headquarters. The professionals had their way blocked, predictably. Bev was outraged.

'Right, then,' he said. 'If my honest pros can't go onto the field through our gate, the amateurs will go through theirs.' And that was what happened.

Was it some kind of political statement from someone whose public utterances had already made him anathema to a number of influential people in cricket? Was it genuine idealism from someone sick of the enforced segregation that persisted in the game? Was it another manifestation of his innate showmanship?

Bev Lyon was a quintessential democrat. He may have been invited to some of the best soirees in town. Head waiters dropped everything to guide him to the best table. His manners had been moulded at public school and the suits he wore were hand-stitched. But he often seemed happiest of all playing poker with his pros or bundling them into the yellow Rolls to celebrate a fight-back at The Oval. 'We just didn't know where he was going to take us,' one doting Gloucestershire player of the time told me, 'until he shouted to his driver . . . The Dorchester!'

An employee at Rediffusion in those early Thirties made a rather similar point. 'It was a struggle to establish ourselves and we worked long hours, six or even seven days a week. But Beverley, as he was known, was liked by everyone who worked for him. He commanded tremendous loyalty. At a time when there couldn't have been a lot of spare cash, he suddenly awarded the whole of the staff at Newcastle a £10 bonus. Office girls as well as highly trained engineers. No question of any discrimination.'

But back to the cricket. The professionals were in considerable awe of him. They didn't agree with all his whims and some of the more intrepid declarations. Ironically, that most independent of spirits, Charlie Parker, whose criticisms were expressed in a stage whisper intended for the captain's ear, could be contrary enough on occasions to take a diametrically opposed view. I am thinking of what happened at Worcester.

The Gloucestershire wickets were tumbling to spin and Parker, watching with his pads on, next man in, couldn't wait to get his manipulative fingers round the seam. 'Go on, skipper, declare now - I want a go at those buggers tonight.' His language was seldom modulated, certainly not when he was talking about the other side. Lyon had a warm regard for his older pros but he didn't approve of them making the decisions for him. He shook his head - and Parker, mumbling to himself, strode to the wicket. 'Bloody Bev Lyon . . . what's the point of ferkin' around out here. We don't need no more runs.'

He didn't take guard. He swung contemptuously at the first ball and missed it by a mile. It also narrowly missed the stumps. The swipe and the miss were repeated for the second ball. Charlie seemed to be saying: 'Bowl a straight one, can't you - I'm not hanging round here all day.' By now he clearly had little regard for the bowler's accuracy. With a sudden gesture, that must have been both fearsome and comical, he swung his bat in an extravagant backward arc and knocked all three stumps out of the ground. He looked challengingly in the direction of the pavilion. Bev found it all too funny to be considered an act of insubordination. He called the batsmen in, the innings declared. Nothing was said to Parker. For his part, he took five wickets that evening . . .

The wondrously gifted Parker, disregarded all but once by petty Test selectors put off by the range of his abrasive vocabulary and the chips on his shoulder, was never an easy man to handle. Lyon alone could manage it; there was mutual affection, though Charlie sometimes had an odd way of revealing it.

'Bev had this great facility for lifting you if you were down,' Charlie Barnett once told me. 'That was particularly true in the case of Parker and Goddard if he detected them having a bit of a moan about their misfortunes. I vividly remember the occasion at Cheltenham when we'd lost the Championship. Our heads were down. That night Bev suddenly turned up at my house and took me to his place in the Cotswolds. Croquet on the lawn! It was the perfect tonic.'

Barnett was a public schoolboy who chose to play as a professional, a rarity in those days. More self-effacing pros called him 'The Guvnor' and relied on him as their spokesman when matters of contract needed to be taken to the committee. He possessed an established countryman's social poise and was articulate when confronting a club official about playing conditions that were considered less than satisfactory.

His admiration for Lyon was considerable. 'He had all the confidence and polish in the world - the rest of us learned it from him. He seemed to have social contacts wherever he went, whether it was a swank restaurant or a prize fight. Bev was a great influence on me. I liked the way he did things. He gave the orders but they were always put as a polite request. He reminded me of the style of the Duke of Beaufort when out hunting. Someone might have left the gate open. The Duke would have seen the flaw in etiquette and would have gone over quietly to point it out. He wouldn't make a fuss about it. Nor would Bev.'

Wally also needed tactful handling. He might make a sublime hundred and then station himself in the slips. But Gloucestershire were at times bereft of fast bowlers and whenever Lyon looked pleadingly in the direction of Hammond, the great batsman was inclined to gaze at the ground. He argued that his work was done.

———

No one in the team knew more about the subtleties of psychology than Bev. His cunning is beautifully illustrated in this account of a match when the amiable ever-bronzed Bernie Bloodworth was behind the wickets. He later became the county groundsman and told Graham Wiltshire, not yet the Gloucestershire coach, what had happened at Cheltenham:

Bev threw the ball to Wally but he clearly had to be persuaded. He was still in his 'slippers' and started, with obvious reluctance, sending down gentle military medium. It wasn't what the skipper wanted at all. Then Bev quietly told me to stand back five yards - and Wally found himself having to increase the pace to reach me. Then, after a nod or two from the skipper, I retreated another five yards . . . and another five yards. Wally eventually realised what was going on. He wasn't at all pleased and mumbled angrily that if Bev wanted him to be really fast, then he bloody well would be. He stormed off for his spikes. And his last remark to Bev was that he could get me to stand behind the sightscreen!

In his history of the county, *Gloucestershire Road*, Grahame Parker tells of a match, also at Cheltenham, when Hammond was goaded into a second spell against Sussex. He wasn't in the best of humours and, off a token run, he let one fly. New Zealander Charlie Dacre was keeping wicket and standing up - and he ended the match with a badly bruised shoulder. Combatant glances were exchanged; Dacre and Hammond were never bosom mates. Those who were present said Wally bowled faster than ever before. Perhaps he resented that the rugged Dacre was standing up to him. By the end of Hammond's bellicose spell, during which he took two wickets, the wicket-keeper had retreated. But the extras' total still mounted alarmingly and the hapless New Zealander was much slandered by the occasional bowler, under his breath.

Back in the bar, Lyon would have commiserated with Dacre on his misfortunes, statistical and bodily. Then he'd have gone to Wally and said: 'What a great bowler you *could* be - the greatest all-rounder in the world.' And it was true. Hammond, for his part, couldn't resist such flattery.

There is much to suggest that socially he tried to model himself on Lyon. He, too, bought a camelhair coat (they used to tease Bev that he wanted to look like Noel Coward). He, too, wore the same kind of trilby. He, too, acquired the unusual habit of carrying a blue silk handkerchief, sticking a few inches out of the right flannel trouser. Many, including the perceptive Grahame Parker, noted the way Hammond copied his social idol.

It is time to evaluate Lyon as a player. He had his first game for Gloucestershire in 1921 and his last in 1947. His runs, just under 11,000, gave him an average of 25 and included 16 hundreds. He could hit straight or pull hard; the batting veered to the unorthodox and didn't readily send the chroniclers in search of poetic imagery. The fact was that Bev was always worth his place, unlike a few amateur captains before and after him.

Against Essex in 1930 he scored a century in each innings. He was proud of those, bought teammates and opponents an extra drink and mischievously hoped that brother Dar would splutter on his breakfast coffee as he read the cricket scores.

He was a fallible batsman, often looking too eagerly for runs. He always wore his watch at the wicket. He glanced repeatedly at it in moments of impatience. He was happiest when his batsmen were in a hurry.

His greatest joy was to find himself partnering Hammond. He'd perch on his bat handle to applaud the best of the cover drives. Bev's first century, at The Oval, was when Wally was at the other end. Five years later, in 1933 at Leicester, he figured in what was for

Gloucestershire a record 336-run third-wicket stand. Whether at the crease or at short leg, he talked incessantly to anyone who would listen. There was plenty of engaging chatter that day at Leicester.

As a fielder he would never have been an asset in the deep because of his poor eyesight. The reflexes served him well at short leg, leg slip or silly point. He also had the courage to remain close to a flailing bat.

Lyon's captaincy was generated by his vibrant imagination. He could be crafty, too, in the way of a Painswick poacher. He'd occasionally dupe an opposing skipper, but do it with a gentle smile on the face so that not too much offence was taken. One or two didn't ever quite forgive him for what they saw as a bit of tactical duplicity.

Under him, Gloucestershire kept winning matches - because he dared. He had no truck with the drearily predictable. That was why his county twice got to runners-up in the Championship. It was the nearest they'd got to the title since Downend's famous medic, W.G., skipped surgery for whole summers on end. Life was much more fun for Bev than for Grace: one tongue-in-cheek challenge from silly point to batsman George Gunn was accepted. Bev nominated the stroke - and George played it, irrespective of where the ball pitched. It was great fun for the pair, confusing for the spectators and infuriating for the bowler, the irascible Parker.

For all his levity, in the evening sunshine when there was nothing much at stake, there was no county skipper more mentally alert. His nerve didn't desert him in the extraordinary match with the Australians in 1930. There was never a more thrilling, more tense finish in the West Country. The result was a tie. Lyon had bowled Goddard and Parker unchanged in the second innings.

He thrived on controversy, of course he did. The most quoted incident happened at Sheffield in 1931 when the first two days were lost to rain. Then Yorkshire's captain, Frank Greenwood, agreed to a ruse proposed by Lyon. Both counties would face one delivery only in their first innings and let it go for four byes. They'd declare and go in pursuit of all fifteen points in what amounted to a one-innings match. Yorkshire lost and Greenwood got it in the neck from his committee. Gloucestershire buoyantly won - and Lyon was castigated as a blackguard by those convinced he had a complete contempt for the hallowed game's structure. It led to a change in the regulations.

He could also be cussed, comical as they say in the country. When a declaration went badly wrong, as it did from time to time, players would keep out of his way for half an hour. When the opposition did their best to kill the game by slow scoring, he was known to send down an over of underarm.

Significantly, none of his players would ever say a word against him. It wasn't just that they wallowed in that occasional ride in the back of his yellow Roller or warmed to an amateur captain ready to have a game of cards with them. They actually savoured his little eccentricities. He might suddenly turn the batting order on its head for no apparent reason. Once at Scarborough, after winning the toss, he sent the lower-order batsmen off for a walk along the Front.

His sporadic critics said he made too many conditions. It was perhaps a valid point. He wasn't always available because of his business commitments. He would even send an apologetic note and ask for a substitute until he arrived, straight from work one assumes, at noon. 'Let's get this match over in two days, chaps - got to be back in the office on Friday!' he'd say. No one was too sure whether it was a joke or not.

Apart from his major stake in Rediffusion, he was a landowner with a dashing lifestyle to go with it. He employed a gentleman's gentleman, who laid out Bev's clothes, washed and drove his car, and cleaned his guns. He may have missed the big tours but he went with Cahn to Ceylon in 1936-37 and dominated every reception with his charm.

His death came in the summer of 1970. The announcement in *The Times* made it clear that there would be no funeral as his body had been bequeathed to the Royal College of Surgeons. 'In death as in life for his fellow men.'

He lived long enough to see some of his radical predictions come true. Whatever the old fogeys once said, he was never a charlatan crystal-gazer. If only he'd been still around, as a captain, to enliven the more dire moments of county cricket in the Fifties and Sixties . . .

After he gave up county cricket, Bev Lyon continued to captain the 2nd XI at Bristol from time to time. In a fixture against Hampshire, Gloucestershire's young players put down seven catches before lunch.

Back in the pavilion, half a dozen shy and embarrassed cricketers were surprised to be asked by the congenial skipper what they wanted to drink. They stammered that they would like an orange juice. He eyed them up and snorted. Graham Wiltshire, who was making his debut that day, was then transfixed as Bev knocked back three double gins in quick succession.

The first ball after lunch, the comparatively venerable Lyon, by then into his fifties, marvellously held on at short leg to a fearful swing off a full toss down the leg side. He nonchalantly threw the ball into the air and called in all the young fielders who formed themselves into a semi-circle.

'Now, you fellows, that's the way to hold your catches.' He paused and pondered the earlier fielding follies. 'But what am I to expect if you train on orange squash!'

NINE

BERTIE POORE

Play Interrupted by Boers

———

Poore, Brigadier-General
Robert Montagu.
Born Carysfort, Dublin, 1866.
Died Wimborne, Hampshire,
1938. Prolific run-getter.
Europeans (1892-1914);
Hampshire (1898-1906, 36
matches). Played three Tests for
South Africa against England
1895-96. Fine all-round
sportsman.

ROBERT 'BERTIE' POORE, a professional soldier of some distinction, made his reputation when on leave. It had nothing to do with military ritual or the field of battle. Back from South Africa, to where shortly he'd return for the Boer War, he established in just two months a cricketing career of almost celebrity status.

In late Victorian times, leave at home was a cherished therapy for a great many officers of the Crown. Their lives and circumstances were often nomadic and rootless, artificial and even sybaritic amid the aura of imperialistic guardianship and intermittent unrest and fears of bloodshed. Leave for them meant the renewed embracing of families, a little overdue procreation. For some of the more freewheeling natures, it meant wanton roistering and rogering. For the handsome Major Poore, in his early thirties and married less than a year, it meant a few invigorating, wholesome sporting weeks in the open air.

He had been invited back for a second year to have a few matches for Hampshire. But despite two hundreds for the county in 1898 and preposterously high scoring abroad, sometimes in hastily arranged fixtures of varying standards or ones of little consequence, his name had a largely unfamiliar ring when it appeared in the public prints.

It was subsequently discovered that he'd never had any proper coaching as a cricketer. No great talent or enthusiasm for the game was detected at school. There was little obvious encouragement from his idiosyncratic father, who probably thought Bertie, a man of the British Army, should not be wasting his time brandishing a cricket bat. The rare entries in the father's diary about his son's feats at the wicket seemed oddly perfunctory.

No one is absolutely sure how Poore, the Sporting Major, learned his cricket. The popular belief is that during his service in India, as a young subaltern, he spent long, boring evenings studying those books and pamphlets devoted to the technique of

---

the game. Cricket's grandiloquently expressed theory supposedly became a preoccupation of his at the time of night when his chums were preferring the bonhomie of the mess. It must be said that for all the wordy wisdom of public school masters and the line drawings that accompanied the articles, Bertie appeared to ignore a good deal of this when it came to the practicalities of the crease.

He gripped a bat rather as if it were a musket he was about to hand on with some urgency to point or short third man. This was his stance, in preparation, as the bowler pounded up. The bat, horizontal, its face towards the sky, was an implement of aggression. Others, like Archie MacLaren, also favoured the horizontal-bat style. None of them held it quite like Poore. He stood exaggeratedly upright, as only a soldier could. The moustache bristled; he talked audibly to himself, in anticipation of the ball's likely length and direction, and how he might most proficiently deal with it.

For someone who had taught himself to play, not all was style and elegance. He possessed an enormous reach and he'd worked out, back in India and South Africa, what he could do best. It came unnaturally for him to play back - so he didn't. His cut, quaint and effective, was played off the front foot. Almost all the shots were.

He made his own charts and diagrams on scraps of paper, with the long-range intention - never fulfilled - of making them the subject of a personalised coaching manual. 'All a matter of common sense,' he used to say. 'Find out what brings you most success, and don't bother your head about anything else.'

Out in India against the Parsees, he learned by experiment how to stretch forward a mile to smother the spinners. He had the acute eyesight which allowed him to do the same against faster bowlers, although Sammy Woods in particular rapped him painfully about the thighs once or twice. There was an intense concentration about the way he batted. 'By God, he does it just like a military operation,' a few of his friends and teammates joked. It was a valid observation.

———

Soldiers were taught not to concede ground. Rather in the same way, he commanded his territory at the crease. He took no chances; there was an innate caution about the manner he placed his bat in the path of a good-length ball. Yet he could also, whenever the bowler wavered, strike with enormous, well coordinated power. He could drive through extra cover as exquisitely as anyone in the contemporary game.

The self-acquired technique, ever inclining to the unorthodox, could be highly attractive. He hit straight; because of his reach, he accumulated half volleys without too much trouble and dispatched them, when his eye was in and the mood was assertive, back over the bowler's head. His more improvised shots had been nurtured, by the process of trial, on the matting and dusty wickets of India where he treated every innings as a progressive exercise in self-education.

Spectators would sometimes suppress a smile at a Poore 'special', though the Major was inordinately proud of his repertoire and never for a moment considered any component unworthy of a place in the most conventional manual. C.B. Fry, as versatile and original on the printed page as the sporting field, had a graphic way of describing this 'long limbed, sinewy and powerful batsman'. In his *The Book of Cricket*, Fry wrote of Poore: 'He has a peculiar slicing manner of cutting, treating the ball as if it were a lemon or a Turk's head . . . ' Maybe a trifle over-graphic.

This is, as I have tried repeatedly to imply, not essentially a book about performances on the field, rather about cricketers off it. Yet how can we possibly ignore or take no more than a nominal interest in the two months of late summer of 1899, when his deeds were momentous and, in an age brimming with the riches of great cricketers, he was briefly and suddenly the most discussed player in the land?

Poore was, perhaps above all else, a well organised man. Things were not too good back in South Africa. The simmering animosities held out a sombre prospect of battle. He argued that this was a leave to be enjoyed. For him, enjoyment was a busy, physical diary. There was clearly time to be spent with his new wife, the former Lady Flora Douglas-Hamilton, no more than five foot tall, so dwarfed by him. But, he told himself, there were other things a fit fella had to do.

'What's happening, Bertie?' his fellow officers asked as they strolled the deck of the steamer bringing them home to England.

He pulled his diary from his pocket. Meticulous as ever, he had planned something for almost every day. 'Let me see, now. Few games of polo already lined up, bit of rough shooting. Flora is determined that we go to all the sherry parties. Ah yes, I'll also be competing at the Royal Naval and Military Tournament at Islington or some damned place like that.' And then, more or less as an afterthought: 'Playing a little cricket, too, no doubt. One or two of my chums on the Hampshire committee have been writing to me . . .'

The other officers looked at each other. They suspected Bertie Poore wasn't going to be idle.

In fact, his itinerary was quite extraordinary. Within a mere fortnight he was scoring three hundreds in a row for Hampshire - and somehow finding the time to star for the winning team in the inter-regimental polo tournament as well as triumphing in the best-man-at-arms mounted event at the Agricultural Hall, Islington. We can assume he also embraced some obligatory drinks parties and a few early mornings, out round the hedgerows, with his 12-bore.

It isn't too certain how much net practice he had, if any, when he met up with his county colleagues. He relied on the theory - and a good eye. The early-season greenness of the wickets had largely disappeared when he turned up.

'Where do you want to go in the order, Major?' his captain

asked. It was no time to be self-effacing, not even if it was his first game of the summer in England. He felt like runs. 'No 3 would do nicely. And-ah call me Bertie.' The pros wisely stuck to Major.

He arrived punctual and freshly-creased at Portsmouth. The game's protocol and marked social scale came naturally to him as an officer. Somerset's bowling was also, it seems, something of a formality. The extrovert Woods was fiery but all over the place. They also had a bowler, Nichols, who was supposedly better at writing plays. Poore played like a soldier, relaxed on leave, glad to be out of uniform. He began with exaggerated caution and then emerged to parade his uncompromising off drives. His innings brought him 104 and 119 not out.

'See you at Southampton for the next fixture, against Lancashire, Bertie. At No 3, of course.'

This time he scored 111 in the first innings, and before the end of the month, back at Portsmouth where the brawny matelots on the boundary led the applause, he made 175. In between, he'd been off playing his polo and excelling in the best-man-at-arms event.

But for someone who had in effect taken up the game late, almost by accident or out of boredom back on the sub-continent, cricket now appeared to be his predominant passion. He went off with the Hampshire team to Taunton for the July 20-22 match, assured that the food was excellent at the Castle Hotel and that the county ground there was shimmering with runs. His response was a breathtakingly assured innings of 304.

It would be churlish to dwell on the fact that Somerset's ecclesiastical wicket-keeper Archie 'The Bishop' Wickham might have held onto a catch when Poore was four. He preached a fine sermon at Martock and may, in moonlighting guilt, have been working on the text for the coming Sunday. Let it be remembered, and marvelled at, that he did not concede a single bye out of

Hampshire's total of 672 for seven. Eventually he caught the Major after Ted Tyler, Farmer White's tutor, beat him with flight.

Hampshire won the match by an innings. The mere result is dwarfed by the feat of Poore. He had already revealed his penchant for laying into the Somerset bowlers. Some of them he had first met when they toured South Africa under Lord Hawke. One of the others, the wan-looking spinner, Beaumont Cranfield, was left wishing he was back humping coal for a winter living in Bristol.

Poore was in magnificent command. Four wickets were actually down for 63 when Teddy Wynyard, another military man, came in to join him. Between them they added 411 in less than four and a half hours. Local shopkeepers heard what was happening, bolted the doors and wryly came to watch. The partnership is still a Hampshire record.

Suddenly this big, handsome army officer was the most discussed batsman in the land: and until June he had been little more than a vague name on the sports pages of the more august newspapers, a part-time cricketer and skilled horseman. In those two almost surreal months with Hampshire, he scored 1,399 runs (average 116). He topped the national averages, was an automatic choice for *Wisden's* 'five of the year' and looked, amazingly, near to Test selection.

The romance couldn't quite be sustained. He played for the Gentlemen at The Oval and Lord's - and, by his standards, failed. In any case, he had an early, untimely and unsporting appointment with the Boers.

There was probably an inevitability about his becoming a soldier. But the Poores also had clerics in the family. Bishop Richard built Salisbury Cathedral. Bertie himself could demonstrate a straight-laced, pious nature. His little homilies from the Bench, when eventually he sat as a Justice of the Peace in Dorset, were strong on Victorian virtues and a rigid code of morality.

—

The strong family influence, like so many of that social station then, was still the army. A number of the Poores had died bravely in battle. Bertie's father had been a major in the 8th (King's Royal Irish) Hussars. One detects more than a few clues of endearing eccentricity, hypochondria and even a sense of grievance in the family records. 'He was somewhat fortunate to live through the first six months of his life, for during this period he fell out of bed and had a foot badly scalded (1834)' . . . 'Suffered from severe rheumatism (1853)' . . . 'Was sick on leave on the recommendation of successive medical boards, during which time he was twice passed over for promotion (1854)' . . . 'His case was pronounced as incurable (same year)' . . .

In spite of his ailments, he went on to receive special mentions for gallant conduct. He had sailed with the 8th Hussars for India in 1857 and distinguished himself at the battle of Kotah-ki-Serai where he started out as second in command and ended as the officer in charge. There is an entry, eloquently sparing of opinion, in the same records: 'For this engagement, three V.C.s were given and balloted for (one officer, two rank and file), the balloting being by rank - officers for officers, sergeants for sergeants etc. Captain Poore recorded his vote for his senior officer, who in consequence received the coveted decoration.' One can only conclude it might more fittingly have gone Poore's way.

Bertie was the eldest son. There were four brothers and three sisters. By the age of twenty he was a lieutenant in the 7th Hussars and on his way to India, where he stayed for nine years, latterly as ADC to the Governor of Bombay, the 4th Baron Harris, who surely stirred young Poore's so far latent regard for cricket more than those dreary textbooks.

Life could be quite splendid: privileged and exotic. He starred in the inter-regimental polo teams, prompting more sympathy for the sweating ponies acquired to carry his weighty frame than for the oppositions. He was a naturally brilliant mounted swordsman. He won the singles and doubles tennis tournaments at Bombay, Poona and Bangalore. He was the best at racquets. They found him a mount in the 1893 Bombay Point-to-Point: and of course, he won. In the regimental contests, no one could remotely match him with a sword or a revolver. Social life enveloped the officers. Poore, good looking as he was and much admired by rich planters' daughters, preferred gymkhanas to dances.

He also accepted the occasional invitation to a tiger-shoot or the more esoteric pig-sticking. An article, 'The British Officer at Play', in a contemporary magazine specifically mentions the sporting versatility of Major Poore. Pig-sticking was listed second only to polo in the eyes of many officers stationed in India:

> Whenever the opportunity presented itself, an officer would put on one side the sterner duties of life to accept an invitation to visit the forests of some friendly maharaja, and would enter into the spirit of the sport with zest. In the estimation of many, there is nothing to be compared to hunting the wild hog on horseback with spear in hand, for it possesses that element of danger which adds piquancy to the sport.

There is no lingering evidence of what Poore made of such a diversion; nor, indeed, of the occasional tiger-shoot which he attended. One is drawn back to the same publication of the times:

> No sportsman worthy of the name, while with his regiment in India, fails to take advantage of the opportunities to go tiger-hunting. If pig-sticking is exciting, it can be imagined that a tiger-hunt raised the blood to boiling point . . . Think of the sportsman perched in a tree, not knowing whether the enraged tiger, roused from his lair by native beaters, will make a dash his

way - giving him chance to get a shot home. You can appreciate the intoxicating pleasure produced by hunting the man-eater. But a tiger is not the only possible item in the bag. By way of variety, bears and jungle-hound, to say nothing of lesser game, fall to the gun of the soldier-sportsman . . .

This gives us an evocative impression of what officer-class army life was like in India. There was clearly much leisure, many invitations from those friendly maharajas.

But beyond the shoots, what sort of soldier was Poore? He could possess a bristly manner, barking the occasional order in a clipped voice guaranteed to cause every private within earshot to cower momentarily. Those who served under him also respected the unambiguity of his style, the basic fairness in his sense of discipline. He demanded, like all the officers, that his uniform was freshly creased and the horses were ready. Any dilatory attitude on the part of a groom brought out the intractable qualities of the martinet.

In the autumn of 1886 he was an emergent lieutenant in the 7th Hussars, not seen by everyone around him as quite the ideal build for the light cavalry. That was a mere technicality. It took him ten years to become a captain and another five to be major. By the start of the 1914 war he was colonel, followed by brigadier-general twelve months later. He left the army in 1921.

Poore saw no active service until he moved to South Africa from India. In 1896 he was much involved with the Matabele Campaign: at the sharp and pragmatic end. He was sent out with a patrol of forty men, with supplies to last them for only four days. They were away from base for more than a month. 'We were reduced to eating the horses,' he would recall years later, distaste still in the voice (and the mouth).

The next year it was the Mashonaland Campaign. This was

when he revealed improvised skills as an enforced medic. A soldier's leg had to be crudely amputated, and Captain Poore volunteered to administer the chloroform.

Throughout the Boer War, he carried the local rank of lieutenant-colonel; he took part in actions in Orange Free State and Transvaal, was mentioned in despatches three times and awarded the DSO. His military career and standing had now been firmly established. In 1911, he commanded the 7th Hussars at the Opening of Parliament by George V, when his regiment lined the streets of London. Four months later he commanded the 7th Hussars at the Coronation, riding in the glittering processions. He served in India and elsewhere during the 1914-18 war, in command of the Jhansi Brigade, and was awarded the CIE.

We've mentioned Poore's administrative skills. He loved planning, putting his ideas on paper, minimising complex military bureaucracy. Records show that while in command, he 'invented and organised a system of instruction which was known in India as the Jhansi System, counterbalancing the shortage of instructors due to the calls of the Great War and considerably speeding up the training.'

Such a bare statement only intrigues. One would like to know more. Yet it is given utter credence in the case of an intensely private and organised man who was said to have acquired at least some of the rudiments of the game of cricket from words and sketches in a textbook, and who could summarise with enviable dexterity the logistics of a leave in England which took in everything from partridge shooting to country-house parties or, in midsummer, tennis tournaments to keenly competitive polo matches.

All that and cricket, too. We can only marvel, one hundred or so years on, at the infinite ease with which Bertie Poore achieved so much. But for his soldiering, he would have played for England

and maybe even have revised the record books by a few more monumental deeds.

No one knows for sure how many runs this self-taught Victorian sporting icon scored. At a time when we can only conclude that he was still getting the hang of it, he hit six hundreds in seven innings in India. Centuries became commonplace for him - and it would be churlish and small-minded to disparage their worth because of the suspect substance of the opposition on some occasions. Almost every time he played, he made a big score. This novice cricketer, who'd learned the game quite outrageously by theory (and doubtless an encouraging dig in the ribs by Lord Harris) monopolised every match in which he took part.

When his regiment went to South Africa, much of the cricket was of a higher standard. He simply carried on. Two of his hundreds were for Natal against Lord Hawke's touring team of 1895-96. It was the only time anyone got to three figures against the tourists. 'Pity you're not a Yorkshireman - I'd bring you back and have you in my side,' said Hawke.

National qualification was apparently no problem and Poore found himself, inevitably on current form, in the South African Test side against Hawke's team. Ironically, the sheer romance of his elevation was not reinforced by performance. 'Test' status should never really have been granted the series, of course. England won twice by an innings. Poor Bertie had not played in such one-sided matches before. By 1897, in Natal, he was back in his element. He scored seven hundreds in a thoroughly predictable row.

We shall never really know what this commanding giant might have achieved with regular county cricket in England. Would his 'theoretical approach' have allowed him to make runs prolifically on the damp, green wickets in April and May? Would wily county pros, nursing their complexes and furnace-hot cricket balls in impatient hands, have in time found a regular way past that ever lunging-forward and cautious bat?

He played in all only thirty-six matches for Hampshire. The Boers, among others, saw to that. Back in England, out of uniform for ever, that analytical mind became increasingly fascinated by the coaching aspects of the game. He put up a net on his lawn. He tutored the local Dorset and Hampshire boys. By now his voice was much more mellow; the village lads at Broadstone viewed the Brigadier-General with genuine affection. Just occasionally he forgot himself and bellowed an order. Then he'd change his tone at once and place a paternal arm round the young cricketer in his plimsolls.

Poore wasn't so far short of sixty when he pulled out his pads and at the affable behest of the MCC played in a civilised West Country tour. He nostalgically hit three centuries in succession. Reluctant to discard his bat for ever, he continued to play in the intermittent village match. A little stiff-jointed perhaps but eager as ever to win and to score runs plentifully. The style had never really changed; in a meadowland of Dorset buttercups, he still pushed distinctively forward, 'nearly as far as the bowler's bloody footmarks' according to the parish wags.

His home was Rose Lawn Coppice, near Wimborne. He'd become Deputy Lieutenant of Dorset and a local magistrate. The leisurely pace by now suited him. Involving himself in the community, he was a governor of several grammar schools and was president of the local branch of the British Legion. He preferred talking about cricket to military matters. Those who lived near him said he was happiest of all watching a village match at Broadstone. He would have liked a son of his own: maybe to work on the angles of the crease that Bertie had so meticulously devised.

Robert Montagu Poore died from throat cancer at the age of 72. Both he and his wife were buried in the kitchen garden of their home, 'under the Brussel sprouts' in a plot of land consecrated by the Bishop of Salisbury. Rose Lawn Coppice was to become the home of his nephew, the Earl of Selkirk.

His dynamic arrival as a county cricketer and all too brief career is marked at the county headquarters by a handsome silver bowl, once presented to Bertie by Hampshire, in the offices. There is surely a case for his on-leave accomplishments to be more openly and proudly displayed. In the villages around Wimborne, the locals talk affectionately of his marvellously pedantic skills and pretend they saw him play.

Some did. During the Fifties, Robin Poore, a nephew, walked into the baker's shop at Colwell near Malvern for a loaf of bread. The baker had never met him before. He took a long look. 'You must be Mr Poore of Coddington Court . . . no mistaking it.' He smiled at his customer's bewilderment. 'I was the Brigadier-General's batman at Gallipoli.'

TEN

JACK MERCER

Bowler with an Ace up his Sleeve

———

Mercer, John. Born Southwick,
Sussex, 1895. Died London 1987.
Right-arm fast-medium bowler.
Sussex (1919-21, 12 matches);
Glamorgan (1922-39, 412 matches);
Northants (1947, one match).
MCC tour to India, Burma and
Ceylon 1926-27.
Became Northamptonshire coach
and then scorer.

IT COULD BE ARGUED THAT I made a serious error of judgment, in the August of 1981 as the scorers were returning to their improvised conclave after lunch at Clarence Park, Weston-super-Mare, by confessing my childlike love of conjuring to Jack Mercer.

We were walking past a row of parked cars. He put his arm on my shoulder and in almost the same motion spirited a pack of cards from his coat pocket. 'You like a trick, then,' he said in the friendly but embarrassingly amplified tones that suggested his hearing aid wasn't switched on. Before I could reply, he had spread the cards, with a deft little flourish, on the gleaming bonnet of a member's Volvo.

I know of entrepreneurs and professional gamblers who unfailingly take handy calculators everywhere with them; of off-duty barbers who always insist on carrying half a dozen combs, which protrude in neat alignment alongside the biros in the breast pocket. These are symbols of their trade. Between innings, batsmen like to stroll the boundary with a cricket ball deep in their flannels: a sort of stage prop to grip in reassuring familiarity when an insensitive spectator starts to tease.

Jack Mercer's props were his playing cards and a back pocket of loose change that he would pull out, at the merest hint of encouragement, to demonstrate his refined skills of sleight of hand. On that early afternoon, at a match when very few of the illustrious players in the Somerset and Northamptonshire sides could fashion many runs on a disturbingly capricious wicket, scorer Mercer showed me three card tricks and another of mesmeric illusion with half a dozen 10p coins.

He accompanied the impromptu performance with some quite urbane banter and a little wink as he detected my genuine bewilderment. What he didn't appear to notice was my increasing concern that he showed no obvious inclination to forsake his singular, appreciative audience and return to his duties in

—

recording the state of the game. By now Lamb and Yardley were back in the middle, fighting their commendable way to half-centuries. Jack Mercer was still making the aces disappear from the bonnet of a Volvo.

That his audience eventually walked out on him was no reflection on either his dexterity or innate charm. I tactfully shouted, mouth to his ear, that I must get back to the press box; he in turn ambled happily in the direction of his temporarily deserted scorebook, to catch up on three missed overs.

I am sure others were similarly privileged, maybe at Cheltenham, New Road or Saffrons, to be doting admirers of this amiable member of the Magic Circle. No doubt kind-hearted colleagues looked after the statistics for him. Occasionally, they did it with a wry smile. Only one or two, with short memories and hearts of stone, ever murmured a real complaint.

Conjuring cricketers used to be quite common in Victorian and Edwardian days. They amused each other on the slow, uncomfortable boats taking them off on tour. They mystified their teammates on rainy afternoons. Their status commanded respect, rather in the way of a village wart-charmer. 'Don't know how you do it, Ciss, but you'm a clever old so-and-so.'

That was Lancashire's Cecil Parkin, usually persuaded to do a few of his tricks when he came to the West Country. They always liked a bit of card magic down in Taunton, where an earlier pro, George Nichols, ran his own concert party, writing the sketches and doubling up as a modest magician. The troupe had a decided cricketing bias. That taciturn and criminally underpraised all-rounder Ernie Robson, born in Yorkshire, managed like so many to shed his shyness on stage. He was recruited for his tenor renditions of the fashionable ballads.

Maybe Parkin, a contemporary of Robson, made the odd guest appearance in the Taunton concert party during Lancashire's visits. Successive generations used still to talk of Ciss's tricks. Perhaps they were simply misled by reports of his bowling variants. He was, after all, the medium-paced off-spinner who when the mood was slightly whimsical - as it often was in his earlier, less embittered days - would offer six different deliveries in an over.

When it came to cricketing conjurers, I suspect that Jack Mercer was the best. Bill Bowes, peering down owl-like through those big spectacles at bewildered teammates, wasn't so far behind. He had plenty of spare time - not of his own choosing - to perfect his dexterity during those wretched days as a prisoner-of-war. Freddie Brown was also captured at Tobruk; he and Bill were to end up fellow prisoners. That was when Brown watched and wondered at the same card tricks, performed sharply but out of a deep sense of boredom. Whenever Bowes and Mercer found themselves together, if on different sides, as players or later as scorer and cricket writer, they pooled their technical enthusiasms for the game and punctuated their conversation with an arcane confidence or two about the apparently latest (still age-old) sleight. There was an additional bond, no doubt, between these two bowling 'wizards'; ironically, they died within days of each other in the late summer of 1987.

If Jack Mercer remained my favourite conjurer of the cricket field it was largely because of the unscheduled pattern of his 'performances'. I suspect that in terms of sheer mystery and showmanship, Fred Castle was at least his equal. He was a schoolmaster in Bath who played for Somerset and once or twice captained them after the last war.

Kent wanted him to become a pro with them. Crystal Palace thought he was a good enough inside forward to play football full-time for them. He pondered a singing career and settled, this notable baritone, for local amateur operatic productions instead. Castle was a popular master who would show boys a couple of simple tricks, on request, after school dinners. Perhaps the biggest mystery of all was how he managed to get time off to play for Somerset during school term. 'Never easy,' he used to tell me. 'Even for my debut against Gloucestershire, a terrific honour for me, I had to write a special pleading letter to the local education authority. I like to think the chairman was a cricket fan.'

Castle retired to Bournemouth, just round the corner from Dean Park. The last time I saw him, he had me in and relented as I gently insisted on a privileged glimpse of his erstwhile skills. He went to a cupboard, undisturbed for some years, and retrieved a dozen or so jumbo-sized playing cards. No close-up magician likes being taken by surprise, when the fingers of old age have lost their suppleness and there is no time for preparation. I can only report that Fred Castle still did the Magic Circle proud.

There remained a delicate and endearing aura of mystery about Jack Mercer. He was apt to withdraw under a veil of privacy in the winter months. He had, latterly, his two homes - one in Northampton, the other in London - but insisted on an unspoken demarcation line. His domestic arrangements were not often a matter of general discussion.

Certainly he liked going to the races. When he went over to the Continent, as he frequently did, the attraction was inclined to be Longchamp where he stood against the rails and bet with modest intuition. On the English courses, he followed his namesake, Joe Mercer, with cussed sentimentality. Cricketers and friends used to say he was a fallible tipster. But he was generous with his whims and hunches. No one would ever dare to say that he lacked generosity of spirit.

Dennis Brookes, that warm-hearted symbol of Northamptonshire cricket, captain, president and gentle fan, retained the greatest of regard for Mercer. Yet he, like so many I spoke to, conceded that through twinkling eyes, Jack remained a bit of a mystery. There was, for instance, his Russian.

He had first gone to Russia in the pre-Revolution days immediately before the First World War. 'Just a holiday with a relative,' he used to say, without much more explanation. But it was an odd and audacious choice for a young Sussex lad. As soon as the war came, he returned to England, joining what was then known as the Sportsmen's Battalion before being given a commission in the Royal Sussex Regiment. He was wounded in France.

Jack was quite a linguist. He could converse easily with either a French officer or, in the years that followed, a bookie at Longchamp. His knowledge of the Russian language impressed everyone, not least the former Worcestershire captain, Phil Neale, one of cricket's rare graduates in Russian. Mercer was known to greet Neale with an animated good-morning in that language. The Brighton sports writer, John Vinnicombe, who spoke Russian like his father - once a *Times* journalist - before him was similarly welcomed before the start of play.

In the last war Mercer worked in intelligence. His sound knowledge of that language was invaluable for translation and monitoring work. 'What did you used to do, Jack?' his mates would ask in post-match intimacy. He'd change the subject, preferring to talk cricket and trading incestuous seam wiles with fellow members of the fast bowlers' fraternity. He was at heart an old charmer who rather relished that enigmatic coating to his personality.

Other cricketers who shared his dressing-room, with Sussex and Glamorgan, and those who witnessed his coaching and then scoring for Northants, all agreed he was a man of notable intelligence. He could knock off the *Times* crossword in five minutes, according to Dennis Brookes. He could carry on a conversation on most subjects. He was an undeniable smoothie when the ladies were around.

The small-minded, who came from a later generation and knew him only in the late Seventies and the Eighties, said they found him something of a bore. That was a facile judgment, as inaccurate as it was petty. He was never a bore. Towards the end of his career as a scorer, his hearing had got progressively worse. That fine cricket writer Matthew Engel, his professional roots lovingly entrenched in Northampton, used to call on Jack several times a year. It was usually a one-way conversation. Jack would point to his hearing aid. 'Not working today.' Who wanted it to be working when Mercer, the beguiling raconteur, was holding court? If you had specific questions to ask him, it was best done on the phone. One ex-Northants player who often shared a restaurant table with Jack in a hotel, recalled: 'It really was embarrassing at times. He didn't realise how loudly he was talking to you - the whole hotel was soon in on the conversation.'

Most of Mercer's cricket was played with Glamorgan. His placid, equable nature was a perfect foil for more excitable Celtic passions around him. The Glamorgan team not only leaned on him for utterly reliable medium-pace; they embraced him without reservation as an adopted Welshman. They too accepted that for all his evident amiability, there was a discernible layer of the unknown about him. 'Not just one but two of them with it in our case, boyo,' they would confide.

And so there were: Frank Ryan and Jack Mercer.

Here were two fine bowlers who could so easily have played for England. No doubt it would have helped Mercer if he'd been with another county. Ryan perhaps needed rather more: a different lifestyle and temperament.

He, like Mercer, was intelligent and prepossessing. Some in those days between the wars used to say he carried himself like a Guardsman who wouldn't have looked out of place in a prestigious sentry-box. Such a deferential role wouldn't have done for him. He was self-contained, a worldly man who had spent some time in North America, though not many were too sure what he had been doing out there.

Frank Ryan, born in New Jersey and educated at a grammar school in Bedford, was a slow left-arm spinner who was almost unplayable when the mood was right. At times it was anything but. He could be fastidious about the way he should be used. Successive skippers knew they were always likely to have a few problems with him during a summer. 'When he was getting a bit of punishment and was visibly not enjoying himself, he was apt to break down with back trouble in the middle of an over.'

The Glamorgan history books refer to him as 'an erratic genius'. He had twenty or so matches with Hampshire before sweet-talking his way into a free lift to Cardiff. He never had too much spare cash. He was seldom without a pretty woman's company or a pint of ale. That was probably where the money went. But he stayed with Glamorgan from 1922-31 and took 913 wickets.

Mercer and Ryan often carried Glamorgan when it came to the bowling. They were two cricketers out of the rut. Ryan was, on his best days, a delightful companion. He was also, of the pair, the likelier match-winner. When he bowled Bradman and had Victor Richardson bamboozled and stumped during a teasing 6 for 21 spell against the Australians at Swansea in 1930, the St Helen's spectators were chanting that he should be put straight into the Test side. 'And Jack Mercer while you're about it.' In that same game with the tourists, less spectacularly it is true, the latter bowled beautifully to take 3 for 70 in just under thirty-three overs.

That exemplified his approach: stamina and unflagging accuracy. And, of course, a good deal more. He was the perfect model for all talented bowlers whose tendency was to hurl the ball at the other end, to the exclusion of control and subtlety.

Mercer had the kind of balance and effortless action that everyone envied. One cannot believe that he ever broke into a sweat. There was too much sheer dignity to allow for such overt signs of physical labour. He stayed with Glamorgan for eighteen seasons and took 1,460 wickets for them. He did it entirely without fuss.

As an eighteen-year-old he had dutifully and optimistically gone to Hove for a few months in search of a cricket career. The war put an end to that notion. He turned up again in 1919 but sensed he would never be more than a shadow of Maurice Tate, already firmly ensconced and bracing himself for the first of his thirty-nine Tests. In bowling terms, they were two of a kind. At that point Tate looked the decidedly better prospect - and he was faster.

Glamorgan were emerging at the time. They had a wetness behind the ears and a fetching earnestness to be accepted, without patronising shrugs, as the latest first-class county. Mercer, ever a perspicacious fellow, argued to himself that they were going to need bowlers. He joined them, though he didn't establish himself in the side until 1925. Two years later he was one of *Wisden's* 'five'.

Bowling within himself at that thoroughly comfortable pace, he excelled in the art of swing. He could make the ball move both ways. There was, too, lurking behind that marvellous nature, an element of raw cunning. I come back to Dennis Brookes, who 'faced and lost wickets to him'. He remembered graphically the quick turn-over of the arm - and the ball swinging wickedly away. 'But Jack could also conceal a very slow in-swinger. He used to post two or three short legs. One had to play forward to him, the same as for Maurice Tate. Then Jack, the old so-and-so, would hold one back and we gave a catch to one of those short legs.'

He went on to say that Mercer's knowledge on matters of bowling was 'second to none'. Nine times he took one hundred wickets in a season. Always he took them with a gentle smile on his face. The nearest he got to real recognition was the 1926-27 tour to India, Burma and Ceylon. He read about his selection in the continental edition of the *Daily Mail*, while on a brief horse-racing holiday in France with the Northants physiotherapist (or whatever he was called in those days). Jack did also go on a Cahn jaunt to Jamaica; but that was mostly memorable for anecdotes in the best Sir Julian tradition.

Some of Mercer's best bowling performances were achieved on Welsh wickets that were not especially conducive to seam and movement through the air. In tandem with Ryan, medium wobble and slow duplicity, he brought unexpected wins for the fledgling county. There couldn't have been anything more staggering than the way Nottinghamshire were stopped in their lofty tracks at the end of the 1927 summer. In fact, they required only the token victory against Glamorgan to make sure of the Championship. It seemed such a formality that Notts had organised a band to welcome them home.

The trappings of celebration seemed reasonable enough. Glamorgan hadn't won a match all season. There was nothing to suggest that they would find a belated Swansea sparkle. But they did - and the title went to Lancashire. Notts lost an extraordinary match by an innings: the band was sent home. In their second innings, they were all out for 61. It was one of Ryan's good days and that meant he was brilliant. So, even more so, was Mercer.

In just over eleven overs of inordinate craft and challenge, Ryan took 4 for 14. Mercer bowled through; his fourteen overs brought him 6 for 31. He always liked playing at St Helen's where the rugby posts were often left up in the summer and the breezes in off Swansea Bay reinforced his swing. Unlike many new-ball bowlers, he played without a trace of malice. That evening at the St Helen's ground, he was genuinely sorry for the Nottinghamshire players. He told them so individually. Then, quietly satisfied with his day's work and showing no signs of fatigue, he took a brisk constitutional along the Mumbles road, sniffing the salty sea air, before catching the train home.

Cricket was the predominant passion in his nicely organised and quite sophisticated life. But it never became an obsession, shutting out the fun. On the day at Worcester in 1936, his benefit year, when he took all ten wickets he received the congratulations of his teammates with a diffident chuckle.

George Lavis nearly spilled the final catch. Jack was to write about it in the Glamorgan yearbook: 'When the press asked George what was the greatest thrill of his career, he said it was taking that particular catch while I stood in an attitude of prayer. In truth I was betting the umpire six bob to four that George would drop it . . . I was pleased to settle my debt.'

Bowling wasn't always as rewarding for him. At Newport in the last season before the war, Glamorgan and Gloucestershire between them scored 942 runs on the last two days, during which only six wickets went down. Hammond's penchant for the bowlers across the Severn was well known. He'd smoothed and smitten an undefeated 302 against them in 1934. Now at Newport he reached an identical score. Gloucestershire amassed 505 for five in one of their innings in this astonishing match, Glamorgan 577 for four in one of theirs, with Emrys Davies 287 not out.

'What chance do the bowlers have on this bloody track?' was a recurrent question from both sides. In the context of the runs ad nauseam. Mercer had no reason to rebuke himself for his 1 for 105 from twenty-one overs. No doubt there were a few choice oaths from Wilf Wooller who battled away for his 0 for 124.

During his fruitful summers for Glamorgan, some of them threadbare years for a county taking tentative early steps with unproved playing resources, he never once lost his fundamental relish for the game. He would complement his medium-pace with occasional off-spinners in the style of Somerset's Arthur Wellard. He would bat with unorthodox resolve; some of his sixes over the rugby stand at Swansea possessed all the soaring trajectory of a long-distance conversion.

He could not possibly be lost to cricket after the war. In fact, after answering an advertisement, he ended up for thirty-six years with Northants - as coach and then scorer. He was a marvellous bowling coach, as helpful to Frank Tyson as to a wild young speed merchant straight from school. He enthused generously when he came across a schoolboy of undeniable promise. 'Got another Brian Statham here,' he'd say. Everyone agreed that there was no better tutor in the esoteric ways of swing.

As a coach of batsmanship, he was understandably rather less authoritative. He used to stand behind the net and say to Dennis Brookes: 'I can see this little gap between bat and pad.' Then they'd exchange a grin.

I came to know him, in a convivial, intermittent way, only in the days when he was a scorer. Those who knew him better told me one of his favourite expressions was: 'Everything is approximate'. Perhaps this summed up his endearing vagueness. He took life - on the walk from the lunch tent to the scorers' box on festival grounds - at his own contemplative pace. He whistled as he went. Sometimes he was a bit late for an appointment. At one close-of-play, the skipper Jim Watts was waiting anxiously for him.

'Wherever have you been, Jack?' he shouted, none too certain that the hearing aid was switched on.

'Oh dear me, Jim. Terribly weighed down this evening by bowling figures.'

It was a fair point. Northants' attack had been belted pretty savagely in the evening sunshine. The statistics were proving a heavy load to Mercer that day. But he didn't often flap.

As I can confirm, his handwriting, even as he went into his

eighties, was neat and assertive. I never saw him wear glasses; fellow scorers say he never carried a watch with him, possibly some private superstition. 'He was one of the game's gentlemen,' they all seemed to say. Essex's Clem Driver was among his many admirers. Jack was one of the greatest talkers of the scorebox; if it wasn't a confidence about the field placings, it was a supposedly infallible tip for Kempton Park next day.

The box never lacked humour. When tailender Jim Griffiths, the subject of inevitable humour on the circuit because of his singular failure to score runs, was batting, Mercer would make much of a snicked single. He'd allow his pencil a balletic flourish and inform his companion: 'Only one now for his career-best.'

Just occasionally, because it concerned his own specific trade, he'd shake his head at a sloppy piece of fast bowling. On the day one of Northants' overseas players was pitching short and aimlessly, Mercer said with pain rather than reproach in his voice: 'I've a whippet at home with more sense than that.'

Among the scorers, an arcane breed, Yorkshire's Ted Lester was something of an institution, like Jack, and regarded with just as much affection. The two, their lives deeply engrained with the game at its most practical and technical level, got on well together. Once or twice, Ted detected a fleeting rustle of irritation from Mercer. 'He could get just a little cross with scorers who hadn't played the game themselves but professed great knowledge of it.'

To illustrate the point, Ted cited a crucial one-day match involving Northants, when the other side won with a ghastly and lucky four. The other scorer, unable for once to suppress his partisanship, jumped to his feet. 'Great shot,' he shouted.

'No it wasn't. It was a dreadful one,' was Mercer's instant retort. Maybe he was being no more than a partisan himself. That was untypical of him, though it grieved him, as a purist who loved cricket's most poetic skills, to see it being devalued in that crude,

---

pragmatic manner.

For the most part, he was famous for his little kindnesses to struggling players, insistent spectators and curious pressmen. To those who shared the scorebox, too.

Ted Lester told me of how Jack came to discover that he suffered from bad feet, the main reason he'd given up playing after a career of powerful and at times bludgeoning batsmanship at No 4 in an illustrious Yorkshire side.

'What size shoes do you take, Ted?'

'Tens.'

'Perfect. Same as me.'

The next day he turned up with a spare pair of suedes. 'Now try these on - just like carpet slippers. I'm going to let you have 'em.'

Every year after that, when the two met, Mercer would present Lester almost ritualistically with a pair of suede shoes. He would make sure he'd 'broken them in' first. Despite repeated attempts by Ted to pay, Jack refused to take anything.

The old enthusiasms showed no sign of receding. But towards the end of his lingering career as a scorer he would get so carried away with his stories or involved with the technical flaws of the match in progress that he'd forget to record the deliveries. He relied increasingly on his colleagues. One or two veiled complaints reached the county secretary who told Ted Lester: 'It's going to have to be the end for Jack. I'll have to break it to him - but I'm dreading it.'

Ted suggested: 'Ease him out gradually. Still send him to matches where old friends and colleagues like Harry Sharp and myself can keep an eye on him.'

It was a nice thought, reflecting that all too elusive camaraderie, a quality which once used spiritually to take the game of cricket outside the realms of impersonal, mundane sport. Ted's offer, though, was superseded. One day, Mercer walked into the secretary's office, smiled through weary but still twinkling eyes, and said: 'I've decided to give it all up.'

That was something, of course, that he could never do. He still told his priceless stories, still showed boys the grip for the one that went away or came back late the other way; still made the aces vanish. He died on a summer's day in 1987 at the age of ninety-two. No one ever said a bad word about him.

ELEVEN

TOM RICHARDSON

A Game Too Many

————

Richardson, Thomas. Born Byfleet,
Surrey, 1870. Died St Jean d'Arvey,
France, 1912.
Surrey (1892-1904, 305 matches);
Somerset (1905, one match).
Tests: 14. Toured Australia
1894-95 and 1897-98. For a time the
finest fast bowler in England. Took all
ten against Essex at The Oval in 1894.

Somerset's ageing post-war pros, at their most engaging and sentimental after the third rapid pint at the close of play, used to confide that by far their most embarrassing match had been the Bank Holiday one at Bristol in 1951. Most of them said they wished they had never taken part in it.

The plaintive occasion was when Wally Hammond was brought back briefly from South Africa, with the intention of helping Gloucestershire's sagging recruitment drive. He listened to persuasive voices and agreed to make one last token appearance for the county.

He walked out, slower and stockier, to waves of embracing applause. But this eyelid-blink of an innings was a mockery of his bountiful talents. He sparred and missed. The timing was lamentable. Gone was the instinctive coordination, the princely panache. Gone too, symbolically, was the blue silk handkerchief that through his triumphant years he carried, just visible, in the pocket of his flannels.

On that cloudy Bank Holiday in the early Fifties, when austerity was reluctant to go away and the demob suits could still be seen on the boundary, he appeared both silent and sad.

Horace Hazell, born in Bristol, had as a lad regularly walked four miles from his home in Brislington just to watch his idol batting at the county ground. Now here he was, this tubby slow left-arm spinner, getting past the Master's bat almost at will. 'And I wasn't even spinning the ball in those little fingers of mine. I didn't like what was happening. It upset me. I was pitching the ball up to Wally, subconsciously wanting him to show us those wonderful cover drives just once more.'

Yet some will surely claim that Somerset were involved in a match, years before, that was every bit as embarrassing in its own way. This was the last wretched time Tom Richardson, most magnificent and kind-hearted of fast bowlers, played first-class cricket.

He had by now left Surrey and was running a thriving pub, the York Street Wine Vaults, in Bath. It's still there, nowadays called simply the Ale House. His pal Len Braund, another Surrey exile who liked both Bath and a strong drink - had advised him to come to the West Country. Sammy Woods, whose conviviality ensured countless contracts in the licensed trade, pulled the strings.

Everyone assumed Tom's cricket was over. He had left The Oval, where for years the adulation had been manifested with that marvellous frisson whenever he set off on his run-up of gathering momentum, rounded up with that little distinctive leap. Now he was putting on weight, finding it hard to resist the ritualistic 'And have one fer yerself, Tom' as he pulled the pints for his customers.

He turned out in a hospital charity match for Bath District against the Rest of the County. Sammy got him for a duck. And he got Sammy. One can only speculate on the extent of the pre-match jollification.

Tom was a celebrity. The members of the Bath Association CC in North Parade, just down the road, vacated the Mason's Arms and went into the Wine Vaults out of new-found loyalty on a Saturday night. Their thirst belied their temperate YMCA roots. 'How about a few overs for us next week,' they'd say amid the bar-room banter. He had given away most of his kit but he was persuaded to play, just occasionally. One of his less exalted teammates used to watch with fascination the way Tom would come in at the close, peel off his shirt and dip the whole of his head into a bucket of cold water. The memory was relayed to successive generations of Bath club cricketers.

But Richardson's renowned stamina was beginning to let him down. He didn't mind a few gentle overs at North Parade, now and again, but he was always ready then to slip quietly away into the shade of the trees at third man. The old rhythm and fizz had deserted him; the appetite was on the wane. After all, as we have implied, the midriff was broadening - and rheumatism was increasingly troubling him. The modest tally of club wickets was being earned more by reputation than pace.

'Think I'll call it a day. Must look after the pub, after all.'

It was all the more surprising then, a few weeks later, when the Somerset county selectors (or was it just Sammy?) named him in their side to play the Australians, in July 1905.

His extraordinary inclusion looked suspiciously like a gimmick. There had been no question of his qualifying for Somerset. But the nation had loved Tom, his skills and his demeanour, and now to everyone's astonishment he was back again, supposedly flexing those yeoman muscles against the tourists.

It was the first time the Australians had played at Bath. In the Wine Vaults, just round the corner from the lovely Abbey and virtually within sight of the Recreation Ground, where the match was to be played, the fixture monopolised conversation. Richardson hadn't even been told that he was in the Somerset team. Perhaps, knowing the idiosyncratic methods of Sammy, he wasn't even told till the night before.

When the *Bath Chronicle* came out a day or so later, it resisted any temptation for sentimentality. Instead it printed a brave, penetrative rebuke:

The inclusion of Tom Richardson was a surprise to Bathonians. They do not see him bowling on the North Parade ground now in club matches and presumably it was for this department of the game he made one of the Somerset eleven against Australia.

It was pretty evident that the bowler whose presence was a terror to many batsmen when in his prime must be content to rest satisfied with the abundant honours and glory he has already won on the cricket field. Younger talent should be encouraged . . .

It went on to report on the weather which was 'above reproach' and gate receipts that were 'beyond the expectations of the most sanguine'.

They didn't offer any opinion about whether Richardson's unlikely presence boosted the crowd. But they did say: 'The Somerset bowling was weak and its lack of sting was never more forcibly demonstrated.'

The inclusion of the once great fast bowler was, however charitably you look at it, a monumental mistake. It only showed how bizarre and outrageously autocratic team selection could be in those days. Oh, Sammy . . .

Tom went on as second change. He sweated a good deal more than usual. The leap was a pallid imitation of its vintage athleticism. For thirteen overs he went through the motions, giving away 65 runs and taking no wickets. He didn't often look like doing so. Nor, in fairness to Richardson, did many of the other Somerset bowlers.

The Aussies made 609 for four, of which Armstrong scored 303 not out, and Noble 127. Somerset, with compounded despair, tried nine bowlers. These included Henry Martyn, the wicket-keeper. He at least had the consolation of belting an attractive maiden hundred in the second innings.

As for Tom Richardson, Test bowler and idol of The Oval on many a sweltering London afternoon, he knew at Bath, after only two or three overs, that he should have stayed back in York Street and continued to pull the ale.

Keene's *Bath Journal* surveyed the unchallenged glut of Australian runs, pondered the undisguised groans of the local supporters and reported pungently: 'To be quite candid, the play itself was more than once in danger of becoming monotonous. It was so unusually one-sided that interest in the proceedings was apt to flag.'

On the second day, according to the paper, 'Woods pursued his theory that what a good ball cannot do, a bad one may . . . he sent down a curious mixture of long-hops and full tosses.'

Martyn, maybe the finest wicket-keeper to play for Somerset, found it all too easy taking the ball from Richardson - that was, on the rare occasions he got past the bat. Not so the great Strudwick, of course, in Tom's most productive days. That was when the almost unplayable ball from 'Curly' Richardson was dug into the ground outside the off stump and ended up down the leg side. Wasn't it Herbert Strudwick who wrote: 'He was the fastest and best I ever played with . . . His best friend Bill Lockwood said he himself was never in the same parish, let alone the same street.'

Richardson wasn't yet thirty-five when he played his one match for Somerset. But in truth he was already an old man. The countless overs in the baking heat of Australia and around the domestic circuit - for a fast man he had at times been over bowled - had taken a cruel toll. Some of the boyish amiability had gone out of the eyes. The black, curly hair was thinner, flecked with grey. His home life was beginning to suffer.

He stayed in Bath for another year or so, before becoming landlord of the Prince's Head, at Richmond. The warmth and conversational buzz of the bar appealed to him. He also had the strength to help lift the big barrels down to the cellars.

By now his wife had left him, conceding custody to him of the three children. He didn't make a great deal of profit from his pubs; perhaps he was too generous in matters of a reciprocal round or two. The hours were long and he slept badly. In 1912 he argued he had earned for himself a short holiday in France with a couple of friends. And that was where he died, in circumstances that remain mysterious even today.

His body was found by villagers on an undulating hill path on 2 July. They realised he was dead and carried him on their shoulders to the nearest *mairie*.

Now come the nagging strands of uncertainty. Why was there no sign of a death certificate or medical records? Was there an inquest as surely there should have been, even by the less rigid legal standards of provincial France? What became of the couple with whom he was holidaying? And why was he found six miles from Aix-les-Bains, where it is quite possible he went to visit the spa in search of a cure for his incipient rheumatism?

A subscription started by a sporting publication in this country ensured that his embalmed body could be brought back. When a dignified funeral service took place, the simultaneous Gentlemen v Players match was respectfully halted. Newspaper reports described the profoundly moving scene at The Oval: the vast field devoid of players, the flags at half-mast. There were tears before play was resumed. Many expressed the sentiments, later to be found in Pentalow's *Cricket: A Weekly Record of the Game*: 'Not only a great bowler, a fine fellow, a man among men . . . with a heart as big as his outward appearance suggested . . .'

Ever since, it has been impossible to ignore the mystery of his death. For years the whisper was that he had killed himself. The rumours were fanned by fellow cricketers, old friends at The Oval and those of his pub customers who dispensed unsubstantiated gossip. They said that for someone of his age he was badly overweight and probably drinking too much. They said he was a lonely man, missing his wife. Certainly the severe bouts of rheumatism were making his life a misery. His face was puffed; there was a weary sadness about the dark, Romany eyes.

By diligent research and calm analysis, Ralph Barker took a detailed look at the circumstances in his excellent book *Ten Great Bowlers*. He, too, was confronted by the sketchiest of contemporary evidence - and the inevitable riddles of the death of a relatively fit man at the age of forty-one.

Mr Barker went back over the last weeks and days in the life of Tom Richardson. He contacted the French authorities once again in the vain hope that additional facts might be discovered on record. None really were. Everything pointed to a death by natural causes. 'Honest Tom' apparently died from a brain haemorrhage while walking on his own at St Jean d'Arvey.

His research, Mr Barker wrote, proved 'beyond all reasonable doubt' that Richardson did not commit suicide. But the dark theory will never go away completely. As recent books have reminded us, an alarming number of first-class cricketers have killed themselves. The chilling division between the visible joy and animation of the game and cricket's nagging mental torment cannot be ignored. Cricket, like no other sport, entraps sensitive souls. Tom, as everyone who played with him said, was among the most sensitive of men. If he had private worries he kept them to himself. His eventual decline and departure from the game were psychological burdens he found difficult to bear. He now accepted he was no longer a particularly fit man. He must have read about and pondered the self-induced deaths of great players like Arthur Shrewsbury just a few years earlier.

Many of his fellow pros found it impossible to believe that a man once so full of fellowship would have contemplated taking his own life. Some reluctantly accepted the rumours but, out of a sense of loyalty, did their best to divert the conversation whenever it turned to Tom. It is probably charitable and right to support Mr Barker's conclusions.

Richardson came from gipsy stock. It revealed itself in the strong, swarthy face and eyes as black as another 'nomad', W. H. Davies, the Super Tramp poet. Did Tom's roots indicate a restless nature? One finds it hard to believe. As a fast bowler, he was mild-mannered and gentle to a degree. 'Hate the buggers more,' other artisan pros would say to him. He couldn't: he never once gave a debutant batsman an unfriendly ball to start him on his career. Once in a match at Scarborough, the ball reared up and hit the batsman, Yorkshire's Ted Wainwright, on the head. Richardson's reaction was one of horror. He rushed down to Wainwright's side. 'It wasn't my fault - it was the wicket,' he told him with almost imploring naïvety.

There were a few minor contradictions in his manner. Meek and acquiescent he may often have appeared. But his innate sense of justice could occasionally surface with alacrity. He would stand up for a fledgling professional who was being given an uneasy few minutes by a patronising senior in the dressing-room. And there was, of course, his courageous stand in the Professionals' Strike of 1896.

None of the Surrey committee had ever envisaged him in any way as a militant. Most of the game's polemics usually passed him by. But he considered it was quite wrong that winter wages should be reduced from thirty to twenty shillings a week. He also shared the concern at the amount of money that was being made - with too little consideration for the professionals - out of extra representative matches against the tourists, as well as the Test fixtures. In the August, the Test selectors were told that five of the team (Abel, Hayward, Richardson, Lohmann and Gunn) wanted £20 each for the match. They had been paid £10 for the Lord's and Manchester Tests.

It should not be forgotten that Richardson and Lohmann had bowled out the Australians for 53 at Lord's. Now the pros in general were in a mood of simmering anger; they wanted a better deal. There were threats 'to withdraw labour'. It infuriated cricket's establishment. In fact, Richardson withdrew his strike demand and played in the August Test. Lohmann's letter, somewhat fawning in content, arrived too late. He never played for England again.

Tom Richardson had arrived at The Oval in 1890, initially to

—

make no great impact and to go on taking weekend wickets for Mitcham instead. He made his debut two years later and went on to claim 2,105 wickets. A great many of his victims were bowled. Above all he bowled at the stumps; there was never a wastage of energy. And, of course, he bowled very fast indeed.

He was directly compared, in terms of basic pace, with Kortright. In the interminable debate about our best fast bowlers of all times, he still comes high on the list. The sheer pace took some of his opponents by surprise in his early days of county cricket. There was even carping comment, from the Trent Bridge dressing-room, about the validity of his action. 'This new feller they've got at Surrey - he chucks it. No one could bowl as fast as that by fair means,' a number of his victims choroused. It was becoming quite fashionable to criticise bowlers' actions. In 'Honest Tom's' case, the moans were quite unfair. Significantly, never again through his career, here and abroad, did anyone publicly question the legality of his delivery.

He actually took a wicket with his opening ball in first-class cricket. It was a catch at third man; usually he didn't rely on his fielders. When, by his second year as an established player, in 1893, he was taking 174 wickets, more than 140 were unaided bowling successes.

Tom's progress was spectacularly swift. By 1894 his haul was 196 and he was being invited to join A. E. Stoddart on the Australian tour. He got on well with the amiable, good-looking Drewy Stoddart, and was grateful for the encouragement given him by the England captain. Here, of course, was another sensitive man. One trusts his darker moods and bouts of depression never surfaced on that trip. It was to be a long time before he put a revolver to his head.

Richardson was to have three quite marvellous seasons for Surrey, starting with his 290 wickets in 1895. He had suddenly become something of a heroic figure; schoolboys were trying to ape his run-up and leap. What they could never hope to capture was the way he could whip back the ball from outside off stump. A few batsmen rapidly learned from the folly of offering no shot. Their leg stick had been too easily, comically, removed.

With Bill Lockwood, he made Surrey's the most feared attack in the country. They pounded away at opposite ends, two great bowlers, different of voice, style and temperament. Not everyone agreed as to which of them was the greater speed merchant. Tom was two years younger. He had more stamina and went down less with injury. He was also less self-confident than Lockwood, who as a boy worked in a Nottingham lace factory. He possessed none of Bill's moods.

Most critics were in agreement that Lockwood did rather more with the ball in the air. Some of the great players of the day said that he, on his day, had the edge. It appears at this distance a suspect argument, when you measure Richardson's value as a fast bowler who was prepared to keep going as long as asked, who bowled a fuller length than Lockwood and who not once revealed a flicker of displeasure or petulance when a batsman was taking fours off the edge.

One or two, with a touch of mischief, implied that there was occasionally an element of envy. On whose part? Not Richardson's. He succeeded Lockwood as bowler of the year. But the pair got on well together, like so many county fast bowlers who stalked, and still do, in tandem.

Lockwood chuckled at Richardson's endearing honesty. 'Go on, Tom,' colleagues would say, 'show us how you grip the ball for the one that comes back to knock over the leg stump.'

'Curly' would fidget. 'You know I can't. Just don't know how I do it. Pick the ball up in my hand and aim it at the other end. I don't try to do anything clever. No one's ever told me to hold the ball in a special way.' And he meant it. Just like Maurice Tate, it all came naturally. They didn't need to articulate - or pretend.

Without pretending in any way, Tom took thirteen wickets in a Test match against the Australians at Old Trafford. He took all ten against Essex. He was apt to pick up thirteen against Somerset (who didn't?) or when he came to Cheltenham.

But fast bowlers are expendable. Their glamour is short-lived, compared with the bravura of our finest batsmen.

Tom Richardson's decline was particularly sad. He seemed unable to suspend it. He puffed as he ran in. The thrust had suddenly gone from the shoulders; no longer was the yorker fast and wicked enough. At The Oval, the faithful spectators murmured their apologies on his behalf. A match or two in 1904 and, for Lockwood as well as Richardson, cricket at Surrey was over.

Professional sport has a cruel, unsentimental edge. Tom put on a brave face, rubbing his rheumaticky joints. Already he had a landlord's tummy. The Cricketers Arms, laden with irony, was to be the first of his three pubs.

He was never, as far as we know, a man obsessed with self-analysis. But after the last customer had gone and he had finished polishing the glasses, he returned to an empty bedroom. We can never be certain how painlessly he coped with the surfeit of doubts that encompass so many cricketers when they leave the game for good.

Tom Richardson was a weary man, now looking nearly ten years older than he was. He had bowled too many overs, with never a raised eyebrow of complaint, on those baked Aussie wickets. Fourteen Test appearances and a nation's adulation were long forgotten by the time he made his abortive and fleeting return at Georgian Bath. Again, as when the Surrey and England captains had asked too much of him, he was too decent a human being to say no.

BIBLIOGRAPHY

H.S. Altham, John Arlott, E.D.R. Eagar, Roy Webber: *Hampshire County Cricket - The Official History* (Phoenix Sports Books, 1957)

Bill Andrews: *The Hand That Bowled Bradman* (Macdonald, 1973)

Ralph Barker: *Ten Great Bowlers* (Chatto and Windus, 1967)

Jack Fingleton: *Batting from Memory, an autobiography* (Collins, 1981)

C.B. Fry: *The Book of Cricket* (George Newnes Ltd, 1899)

Glamorgan Centenary Booklet

Grahame Parker: *Gloucester Road* (Pelham Books, 1983)

J.N. Pentalow (ed): *Lord's Cricket - a Weekly Record*

Siegfried Sassoon: *Memoirs of a Fox-Hunting Man* (Faber & Gwyer, 1928)

The Old Century and Seven More Years (Faber & Faber, 1938)

Wisden Cricketers' Almanack

Wilfred Wooller: *A History of County Cricket, Glamorgan* (Arthur Barker Ltd, 1971)

Peter Wynne-Thomas: *The History of Hampshire CCC* (Christopher Helm, 1988)

INDEX

Abel, Robert, 97, 195

Alley, Bill, 121

Altham, H.S., 108, 121

Andrews, Bill, 71-88

Andrews, Ennyd, 72, 76-77, 85

Andrews, Jack, 87

Andrews, Mark, 81, 84

Andrews, Michael, 78

Andrews, Sara, 83, 85

Arlott, John, 25, 54, 56, 70, 75

Armstrong, W.W., 191

Atkinson, Colin, 73, 82, 121

Awdry, Charles, 128

Awdry, C.E., 128

Awdry, Col R.W., 127

Barker, Ralph, 193

Bannister, Alex, 73

Barbour, Joyce, 95

Barbour, Dr Tony, 96

Barnett, Ben, 49, 67

Barnett, C.J., 151

Bedser, Alec, 99

Bedser, Eric, 99

Benaud, Richie, 68

Berry, Scyld, 70

Bird, Richard, 95

Bloodworth, Bernie, 152

Blunden Edmund, 39, 51

Botham, Ian, 84, 125

Bowes, Bill, 133, 174

Boycott, Geoffrey, 56

Bradman, Sir Donald, 54, 58-61, 70, 178

Bradman, Jessie, 62-63

Braund, Len, 108, 115, 189

Brookes, Dennis, 175-176, 179, 182

Brown, F.R., 174

Burnett, A.E., 20

Burrough, Dickie, 80

Buse, Bertie, 86

Cahn, Sir Julien, 131-132, 156, 180

Cardus, Sir Neville, 67-68

Carter, H., 98, 119

Castle, Fred, 174

Chapman, Percy, 140

Chappell, Ian, 60

Chester, Frank, 131-132

Chidgey, Harry, 109, 119

Clay, J.C., 20

Cleese, John, 86

Close, Brian, 113

Compton, Denis, 60, 125, 126

Constantine, Sir Learie, 25

Corrigan, Peter, 69

Cowderoy, Daphne, 90, 92, 94

Dacre, Charlie, 152-153

Daniell, John, 73, 108, 113, 147

Davies, Emrys, 181

Davis, Roger, 34-35

Denness, Mike, 69

Denning, Peter, 70

Denning, Tom, 70

Dexter, Ted, 25

Dipper, Alf, 146

Douglas, J.W.H.T., 116, 120

Dredge, Sam, 41

Driver, Clem, 183

Ducat, Andy, 89-104

Ducat, Vera, 91, 94

Earle, Guy, 147

Eastman, Laurie, 146

Edrich, Bill, 69, 136

Edwards, Bill, 20

Ellis, Tony, 86

Engel, Matthew, 177

Evans, Harold, 68

Farnes, Ken, 134, 141

Fender, Percy, 99, 133, 142-143

Fenner, George, 133

Fingleton, Belinda, 58, 65

Fingleton, Jack, 49, 53-70

Fingleton, Philippa, 57

Forrester, Reggie, 128-129

Fry, C.B., 103, 148, 160

Gearing, Bill, 39

Gimblett, Harold, 76, 83, 108, 113

Gloucester, Duke of, 94

Goddard, Tom, 131, 141, 147, 151, 154

Goodland, David, 117

Goodland, Gill, 107, 112, 118

Gower, David, 24

Grace, W.G., 154

Green, Sir Hugh Carleton, 56-57

Greenwood, Frank, 155

Gregory, J.M., 98, 119

Greswell, Charles, 114

Greswell, Doris, 116

Greswell, Ernest, 114, 118

Greswell, John, 112, 117

Greswell, Rachel, 112, 116, 117

Greswell, W.T., 105-122

Griffiths, Jim, 183

Gunn, George, 154

Hain, Peter, 24

Hammond, W.R., 33, 62, 77, 132,
    135, 141, 151-153, 181, 188

Hardy, Sam, 101

Harris, Charlie, 32

Harris, Lord, 164, 168

Hartigan, R.J., 119

Harvey, Ken, 132

Hassett, Lindsay, 54

Hawke, Lord, 145, 163, 168

Hayes, E.G., 98

Hayward, Tom, 96, 195

Hazell, Horace, 74, 80, 188

Henderson, Bishop 'Jock', 50

Hitch, Bill, 93

Hobbs, Sir Jack, 93, 96-97, 104,
    107, 116

Hollies, Eric, 134

Hollis, Christopher, 40

Holmes, E.R.T., 134

Howell, Lord, 25, 66

Howorth, Dick, 26

Hungerford, Lord, 44

Hunt, George, 107, 119

Hutton, Sir Leonard, 60, 113

Iddon, Jack, 134

Ingle, R.A., 80, 86

Jaques, Arthur, 103

Jardine, Douglas, 141

Jewell, Major M.F.S., 146

Jones, Willie, 27

Jupp, Vallance, 79

Kinneir, Septimus (Paul), 126

Kitley, Jim, 39

Knox, Ronald, 40

Kortright, C.J., 196

Lamb, Allan, 173

Larwood, Harold, 57-58, 60, 141

Laver, F., 119

Lavis, George, 181

Lester, Ted, 183-184

INDEX

Lewis, Tony, 34-35

Liddell, Ned, 102

Lindwall, Ray, 60

Lock, Bert, 63

Lockwood, Bill, 192, 197

Lohmann, George, 195

Longrigg, E.F. (Bunty), 121

Lowry, Tom, 36

Luff, John, 50, 62-63

Lyon, B.H. (Bev), 139-156

Lyon, Jeremiah, 146-147

Lyon, M.D. (Dar), 146-148

Lyttleton, Hon Charles, 26

McAlister, P.A., 119

McCabe, Stan, 54

McDonald, Ted, 74, 98

McGilvray, Alan, 56

MacLaren, Archie, 159

Makepeace, Harry, 116

Mann, George, 33

Marlar, Robin, 69

Martyn, Henry, 191-192

Menzies, Sir Robert, 65-66

Mercer, Jack, 26, 171-185

Mercer, Joe, 175

Meyer, R.J.O., 86, 113

Miller, Keith, 60

Milton, Arthur, 27-28

Neale, Phil, 176

Newman, Roy, 42

Newton, Arthur, 109, 117

Nichols, George, 162, 173

Noble, Monty, 119, 191

Oakes, Charlie, 138

O'Connor, Jack, 146

O'Reilly, Bill, 60, 70

Paine, George, 134

Palairet, Lionel, 83

Parker, Charlie, 150-151, 154

Parker, Grahame, 152-153

Parkhouse, Gilbert, 20

Parkin, Cecil, 173

Parkinson, Michael, 61, 66

Parks, J.H., 138

Pataudi, Nawab of, 141

Peach, Alan, 99

Pearson, Tony, 49

Peebles, Ian, 138

Perrott, Johnny, 46

Poore, Robert 'Bertie', 157-170

Poore, Robin, 170

Pressdee, Jim, 18-21

Reynolds, Henry, 39

Rhodes, Wilfred, 116

Richardson, Tom, 187-198

Richardson, Victor, 178

Robertson-Glasgow, R.C., 55,
    104, 108, 119

Robins, R.W.V., 26, 127

Robson, Ernie, 87, 119, 146, 173

Roebuck, Paul, 50

Roebuck, Peter, 50

Rose, Brian, 81, 85, 88

Ryan, Frank, 177, 180

Salmon, Father Martin, 40, 49,
    63-64

Sandham, Andy, 97-98, 104

Sassoon, George, 43, 51

Sassoon, Siegfried, 37-52

Selkirk, Earl of, 170

Sharp, Harry, 184

Sharpe, Ivor, 92

Shepherd, Tom, 103-104

Sherwood, Robert, 95

Shinwell, Emanuel, 112

Shrewsbury, Arthur, 194

Silk, Dennis, 38, 41-42, 47, 49

Simpson, Reg, 27, 32

Sinfield, Reg, 133, 148

Singh, Swaranjit, 48

Smith, Bill, 127-128

Smith, David, 136-137

Smith, Eli, 124

Smith, Jesse, 126

Smith Jim, 123-138

Smith, Peter, 136

Stackpole, K.R., 60

Stancer, Ernie, 45

Statham, Brian, 182

Stoddart, A.E., 196

Strudwick, Herbert, 192

Swanton, E.W., 68, 76, 108

Tate, Maurice, 103, 179, 198

Taylor, C.H., 100

Tout, Tom, 80

Trafford, Dom Aidan, 39

Trueman, Fred, 18

Trumper, Victor, 68

Tucker, Preb G.E., 121

Turnbull, Maurice, 36

Turner, Bert, 45

Tyler, Ted, 163

Tyson, Frank, 182

Vinnicombe, John, 176

Voce, Bill, 58, 60, 141

Wainwright, Ted, 195

Walker, Billy, 101

Walker, Peter, 35

Walters, C.F., 141-142

Warner, Sir Pelham F., 59, 104

Watts, Hugh, 50

Watts, Jim, 182

Wellard, Arthur, 62, 74, 79-80,
    124, 136, 182

Wheatley, Ossie, 20

White, Crawford, 73

White, Harry, 132-133

White, J.C., 81, 84, 86, 109, 113, 119

Whitty, Bill, 119

Wickham, Preb A.P., 162

Williams, J.P.R., 84

Wilson, Andy, 27-28, 131-133, 136

Wilson, Lord, 66

Wiltshire, Graham, 152, 156

Woodcock, John, 60

Woodfull, Bill, 59, 67, 140

Woods, Sammy, 74, 83, 113, 159,
    189-190

Wooller, Wilf, 17-36, 83, 181

Woolley, Frank, 38, 43, 116

Wotton, Simon, 81

Wyatt, R.E.S., 134-135, 140

Wynyard, Teddy, 163

Yardley, T.J., 173

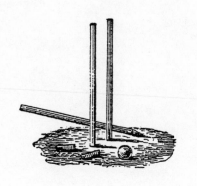